Come, Holy Spirit

*Inner Fire, Giver of Life,
and Comforter of the Poor*

D1557387

Leonardo Boff

Translated by Margaret Wilde

ORBIS BOOKS
www.orbisbooks.com

Founded in 1970, Orbis Books endeavors to publish works that enlighten the mind, nourish the spirit, and challenge the conscience. The publishing arm of the Maryknoll Fathers and Brothers, Orbis seeks to explore the global dimensions of the Christian faith and mission, to invite dialogue with diverse cultures and religious traditions, and to serve the cause of reconciliation and peace. The books published reflect the views of their authors and do not represent the official position of the Maryknoll Society. To learn more about Maryknoll and Orbis Books, please visit our website at www.maryknollsociety.org

Library of Congress Cataloging-in-Publication Data

Boff, Leonardo.
  [O Espírito Santo. English]
    Come, Holy Spirit : inner fire, giver of life, and comforter of the poor / Leonardo Boff ; translated by Margaret Wilde.
        pages cm
    "Originally published as: O Espírito Santo : fogo interior, doador de vida e pai dos pobres. 2013 by Animus/Anima Produoes Ltda., Petrcentpolis, RJ, Brasil."
    Includes bibliographical references and index.
    ISBN 978-1-62698-106-5
    1. Holy Spirit. 2. Spiritual life. I. Title.
BT121.3.B6513 2015
231'.3—dc23

                                                                  2014028548

Contents

Preface

Pentecost Was Only the Beginning

After many years of research and reflection, I offer here a modest treatise on the Holy Spirit: in the cosmos, in humankind, in religions, in the churches, and in every human being, especially in the poor.

We live in dangerous times, which call us to serious reflection on the *Spiritus Creator*. All creation is in danger. The poor and marginalized are suffering great oppression, which calls for a process of liberation. The danger is not from an incoming meteorite, like the one sixty-five million years ago that wiped out the dinosaurs after more than a hundred million years on the earth. Today's meteorite is called *homo sapiens et demens*, with the emphasis on *demens*. With our hostility toward the earth and all its ecosystems, humanity is poised to wipe out human life, destroy our civilization, and inflict terrible damage on the whole biosphere. It has been rightly said that we are living in a new geological era, the *anthropocene*: humankind itself is the great danger to the earth-system and the life-system.

Here we shall reflect on the Holy Spirit in that context, with all the rigor that theology requires. We shall explore history in search of experiences that can help us grasp the spirit. We will find it first in the cosmos, and only then in ourselves.

We shall look beyond that spirit to the Spirit of God, and especially to the Holy Spirit, the Third Person of the Holy Trinity.

Our sources are human experience and the founding texts of the Christian faith: the two Testaments.

Within this effort of retrieval, we are concerned with one especially complex paradigmatic task. To think of the Spirit is to think of movement, action, process, appearance, story, and the irruption of something new and surprising. It means thinking about what we are constantly becoming. These are not things that can be described in the classical concepts of Western, traditional, conventional theological discourse. Our concepts of God, Christ, grace, and the Church were first thought out in metaphysical categories of substance, essence, and natures. They are static concepts, forever circumscribed and immutable. This is the Greek paradigm, officially incorporated into Christian theology.

But to fully understand the Holy Spirit we need a different paradigm, more in line with modern cosmology. A cosmological perspective helps us see the genesis of all things: their emergence out of the Unnamable, Mysterious, and Loving Energy that exists before there was a before, at the zero point of time and space. That Energy upholds the universe and all the beings that have been and will be; it penetrates creation from beginning to end.

To rethink the third article of the Creed—"I believe in the Holy Spirit"—from this perspective is a task fraught with difficulties. We shall put our best efforts into that task, knowing that our efforts will fall short of what God the Spirit requires.

Theological reflection is never the work of one person, but of a community filled with faith, trying to shed light on a dark horizon. We know that this darkness is part of the Mystery. The Mystery is always open to us, but it is also hidden. The theologian's task is an unceasing search for its revelation.

Hiddenness is in the nature of the Spirit. Discovering it is in the nature of human beings. The Spirit blows where it chooses, and we do not know where it comes from or where it goes (John 3:8), but that does not free us from the task of unveiling it. And when to our surprise it breaks through, we rejoice and celebrate. We celebrate with excitement. We are excited and intoxicated by its grace and its gifts.

Pentecost was only the beginning. It spreads through the length and breadth of history, and reaches us in our own time of living and suffering.

Leonardo Boff
Petrópolis, Pentecost 2013

1

⚭

Come, Holy Spirit, Come Soon!

The situation of the world, religions, our churches, and the poor, causes us to cry out: "Come, Holy Spirit! Come soon to deliver us!" The cry arises from the depths of a terrible crisis that can plunge us into an abyss or inspire a qualitative leap into a new kind of humanity: toward a different way of living in our only shared home, Mother Earth.

In this context of fear and anguish, our hearts echo the words of the Pentecost hymn: *"Sine tuo numine nihil est in homine, nihil est innoxium"* (without your grace there is nothing in us, nothing that is not harmful). But another line of the hymn fills us with hope: *"In labore requies, in aestu temperies, in fletu solatium"* (in labor, rest, in heat, temperance, in tears, solace).

The Presence of the Spirit in Great Crises

The Holy Spirit is everywhere in history, but it breaks through especially at critical moments for the universe, for humanity, or for the life of the individual. At the singular moment of the "big bang"—the original upheaval or silent explosion (before time and space, sound could not travel) of that tiny speck, a billion times smaller than the head of a pin, but full of energy and information, giving rise to the universe as we know it—the Spirit was there in its densest form. That is reflected in the first biblical story of creation, describing the wind from God that swept over the original chaos (*tohuwabohu*: Genesis 1:2). It was the Spirit that upheld the delicate balance of all the factors that made possible the expansion of fundamental energies, material (the "God particle" and the "Higgs boson"), and the appearance of the giant red stars. After many millions of years those stars exploded, giving rise to the matter out of which the galaxies, stars, planets, and we were created.

The Spirit was present when that matter reached the level of complexity that made possible the emergence of life, 3.8 billion years ago. It was present in the fifteen great extinctions that later came upon the earth, especially the Cambrian extinction 570 million years ago, when 80–90 percent of all living species disappeared. It was present again in the Permian-Triassic extinction 245 million years ago, when the single great continent of Pangaea broke apart and the continents we know appeared.

It was especially present in the Cretacean age 65 million years ago, when a meteorite 9.7 kilometers wide plunged into the Caribbean and produced a veritable ecological Armageddon, destroying the dinosaurs and most of the other species that had walked the earth for 133 million years. As if to make up for so much destruction, that catastrophe was followed by the greatest blossoming of biodiversity in earth's history.

That was when our first ancestors began to live in the canopy of the great trees, trembling in fear of being eaten by the dinosaurs. From then on the Spirit intensified its presence in a unique way, bringing human beings out of the animal world as the bearer of consciousness, intelligence, and the ability to love and care for others. That mysterious event began between seven and nine million years ago, and a hundred thousand years ago it led to the emergence of *sapiens sapiens*: the human ancestors of today's men and women.

For Christians, the greatest presence of the Spirit was its coming to Mary. It came and never left. That permanent presence led to the holy humanity of Jesus. And with Jesus it became a constant presence in human history, especially through its incarnation in the life of an itinerant preacher and proclaimer of a great utopia:

the Reign of God. By the power of the Spirit, Jesus of Nazareth cured the sick and raised the dead. After his execution on the cross the Spirit raised him, and made him the "last Adam" (1 Corinthians 15:45).

The Spirit was present in the tongues of fire that suddenly came down on the community of disciples of Jesus, fearful and confused, not understanding how someone who "went about doing good" (Acts 10:38) could die on a cross and then rise again. It was present when the disciples, uncertain where to go next, decided to spread the liberating message of Jesus to all the world. "For it has seemed good to the Holy Spirit and to us," they said (Acts 15:28), to turn toward the gentiles.

We could give many more examples of inspiring breakthroughs, made possible by the action of the Holy Spirit. The Second Vatican Council makes the point emphatically: "God's Spirit, Who with a marvelous providence directs the unfolding of time and renews the face of the earth, is not absent from this development" (*Gaudium et Spes*, 26). Four breakthroughs in our own time are worthy of note: the Second Vatican Council, the Episcopal Conference of Latin American Bishops in Medellín, the rise of the Church of Liberation, and the Charismatic Renewal of the Catholic Church.

Vatican II (1962–1965) brought the Church into step with the modern world and its freedoms. In particular it established a dialogue with science and technology, the labor movement, secularization, ecumenism, other religions, and fundamental human rights. The Spirit brought new light into the dark corners of the institutional Church.

At Medellín (1968) the Church began to walk with the underworld of poverty and misery that characterized the Latin American continent, then and now. By the power of the Spirit, Latin American pastors made a courageous option for the poor and against poverty, and decided to implement a pastoral practice of integral liberation: not only from our personal and collective sins, but from the sins of oppression, the impoverishment of the masses, discrimination against indigenous peoples, contempt for people of African descent, and the domination of women that men have practiced since the Neolithic age.

The Church of Liberation was also born through the power of the Spirit. We see its face in the popular reading of the Bible, in the Base Ecclesial Communities' new way of being Church, in diverse social ministries (the pastorals of indigenous peoples, people of African descent, land, health, children, and others), and in the reflection drawn from all of these that we call the Theology of Liberation. This Church of Liberation has shaped Christian commitment to those oppressed, imprisoned, tortured, and killed by military dictatorships. Few churches have been blessed by so many martyrs, lay and religious, priests, theologians, and even bishops like Angelleli in Argentina and Oscar Arnulfo Romero in El Salvador.

The fourth irruption of the Spirit, to which we shall return in greater detail, was the appearance of the Catholic Charismatic Renewal in 1967 in the United States and in Latin America in the 1970s. It restored the centrality of prayer, spirituality, and the charisms of the Spirit by creating communities of prayer and cultivating the gifts of the Holy Spirit. That renewal helped overcome the rigidity of the ecclesiastical structure, doctrinal coldness, and the clerical monopoly on the word, thus opening the way to free expression by the faithful.

Finally, a fifth irruption of the Spirit can be seen in the election of Pope Francis, who came "from the end of the earth," from Argentina in early 2013. With him there emerges another model for exercising the petrine function. He no longer wishes to govern the church on the basis of canon law or in an absolutist style, but instead in charity and collegiality. He has stripped himself of all symbols of power, abandoned the pontifical palace, making his home in St. Martha's Guesthouse where he eats along with everyone else. He prefers to be called "bishop of Rome" rather than "Universal Pope." His name, Francis, is more than a name; it represents the project of a church that is humble, poor, open to all—a type of "field hospital" in which all can be healed. Its center is not the church but the historical Jesus, and its principal mission is not to teach doctrines but to promote the following of the historical Jesus, who calls us to love, solidarity, compassion, and to the unlimited acceptance of all types of people, without questioning their moral, ideological, or religious condition. He is renovating the Tradition of Jesus in tension with the institutionalism of the Catholic religion. His significance overflows the church and is seen as a light for all the world, especially in the defense of the poor, in the critique of an economic system which is, according to him, "evil in its roots" in its lack of solidarity with the suffering peoples of the world. (For a closer look at the mission and vision of Pope Francis, see L. Boff, *Francis of Rome & Francis of Assisi*, 2014.)

These five events can be evaluated theologically only from the perspective of the Holy Spirit. It always acts within history, and with special creativity in the Church, making it a source of hope and joy in faith and life. The Spirit shows itself, in the words of the Pentecost liturgy, as *pater pauperum*—the father of the poor, inspiring them to organize and seek the freedom that society denies them.

Today we may be living through the greatest crisis in human history. It is a very important crisis, because it may be terminal. In effect we now hold the instruments of self-destruction in our hands. We have built instruments of death that may kill us all and destroy our civilization, which has been built over many thousands of years of creative work. A large part of the earth's biodiversity may die along with us. If that tragedy comes to pass, the earth will go on turning without us, covered with dead bodies, devastated and impoverished.

That is why we say that our technology of death has brought about a new geological age: the Anthropocene. Humanity is coming in like a great, destructive meteor, as if we would rather destroy ourselves and the living earth, Gaia, than change our way of life and our relationship with nature and Mother Earth. Like the Jews in ancient Palestine who chose Barabbas over Jesus, the enemies of life today may be choosing Herod over the innocent children he massacred in the region of Bethlehem, where Jesus was born. They are becoming like an earthly Satan, instead of the Guardian Angel of creation.

Now is the time to pray, to plead, to cry out: *Veni Sancte Spiritus et emitte caelitus lucis tuae radium* (Come, Holy Spirit, and send forth the holy radiance of your light).

Without the presence of the Holy Spirit we are in danger of letting the crisis plunge us into irreversible tragedy, instead of being an opportunity for cleansing, purification, and growth.

We who once dared to eliminate the Son of God who wanted to be one of us, by crucifying him, why should we not feel a perverse desire to destroy everything in our reach, including our own future?

But we are convinced that the Giver of life, the *Spiritus Creator*, will "cleanse that which is unclean, water that which is dry, heal that which is wounded" (*lava quod est sordidum, riga quod es aridum, sana quod est saucium*). We shall confront the Anthropocene with the Ecocene (protection of all ecosystems); we shall replace the anthropozoic age with the *ecozoic* age. Instead of the culture of destructive, unlimited growth, we shall offer a culture of sustainable life. We shall replace a material quality of life available only to a few, with the good life which is available to everyone. God, who is described in the Book of Wisdom as the Lord who loves the living (11:26), will not allow life to destroy itself.

The great extinctions of the past did not succeed in destroying life. Life always survived, triumphed, and after thousands of years of evolutionary labor, restored its immeasurable diversity of life forms. Even now, despite our irresponsibility, life will not be destroyed. There will surely be a dark, fearsome, and painful Good Friday, but it cannot block the coming of an invincible, triumphant, and glorious resurrection.

The Erosion of the Sources of Meaning

It has been truly said that human beings are devoured by two hungers: for bread and for spirituality. Hunger for bread can be satisfied, although millions of people are still hungry. They are still hungry because we have turned food, water, land, and seeds into "commodities," that is, products to be bought and sold on the market. That is a sin against life, because everything that sustains life—especially water, which is present in all food—is sacred and cannot rightly be bought and sold. The table is spread with an abundance of food, but the hungry do not have the money they need to buy it. We can satisfy the hunger of the whole world, but we do not do it, because we do not love our neighbor; we have lost our sense of compassion and solidarity with suffering humanity.

But the hunger for spirituality is insatiable. It is a hunger for communion, solidarity, self-giving love, dialogue, and prayer to the Creator of all things. These hidden yearnings never stop growing within human beings. We throb with desire for the infinite. Only the truly infinite can give us rest. We do not find it in today's society, which cares for the material and not the spiritual. Our inner, infinite search is not for material things. That is why our obsession with accumulating and enjoying material goods eventually leads to emptiness and disappointment. We cry out for something greater, more humanizing. And the Holy Spirit is present, hidden behind that something.

This is where we begin to ask about the meaning of life. A coherent sense of life and history is one of the basic human needs. Emptiness and absurdity produce anxiety, a feeling of loneliness and rootlessness. Industrial, postindustrial, and consumer societies, based on cold, calculating reason, have given primacy to individuals and their private interests. Reality became fragmented, social norms dissolved, the sacred became a burlesque, and the great truths—now called "grand narratives," metaphysical essentialism, relics of times past—became targets of derision. The rule today is "anything goes"; different ways of thinking, different positions, different readings of reality are seen as equally valid. We have created a total relativism, in which nothing really matters because nothing is worth the trouble.

This is sometimes called postmodernism; I see it as the most advanced and decadent stage of bourgeois opulence. Not satisfied with tearing down the present, it is also tearing down the future. Its decadence is marked by a total lack of commitment to transforming the world or to improving human life.

This attitude is reflected in a glaring lack of solidarity with the tragic fate of the millions of people who struggle for a halfway decent life, for a chance to live better than animals, with access to the cultural goods that enrich their vision. No culture can survive without a shared narrative that gives cohesion, dignity, honesty, value, and meaning to its collective life. Postmodernity denies the legitimacy of this fundamental yearning.

Yet against all postmodern expectations, people everywhere are finding meaning in their toil and suffering, searching for a north star to orient their lives and open horizons of hope. We can live without faith, but not without hope. Without hope we are a step away from meaningless violence, from the trivialization of death, and eventually from suicide.

But the resources for ongoing production of meaning that we once had are now being eroded. No one—not the Pope, not His Holiness the Dalai Lama—can say with certainty what is right or wrong for everyone, or what is needed at this stage in the history of humanity and the planet.

The global crisis of our civilization stems largely from the absence of a spirituality that shapes a vision of the future, a vision that points to new ways and gives us strength for the hardest times. Such a crisis can be overcome only through a new experience of the essential Being that gives rise to a living spirituality.

There was a time when this fundamental need for human meaning could be met through philosophies and other spiritual paths. But they became formalized and lost their creative vitality. They developed more sophisticated ways of rethinking and rearticulating what was already known, but they lacked the courage to invent new visions, hope-giving dreams, and inspiring utopias. We are in the throes of a "cultural malaise" like the one that brought about the fall of the Roman Empire. Our "gods," like theirs, are no longer believable. And the "new gods" that pop up everywhere are not strong enough to earn recognition and respect, or to earn a place on the altars of the historical process.

The Spirit in History: The Collapse of the Soviet Empire, the Emergence of Globalization, the World Social Forum, and Ecological Consciousness

This is not the place to expound in depth on the complex activity of the Spirit in history. But any such analysis would have to include the Holy Spirit's role in *the fall of the great Soviet empire*, which was rooted in an atheistic state socialism with no respect for individual rights. It is astonishing that the Soviet Union, the second most powerful nation in the world, with the military capability to destroy all humanity, collapsed without going through a violent process of rebellions and civil wars. It began when the Berlin Wall came down in 1989. Then one after another, like a house of cards, the other Soviet republics began proclaiming their independence from Moscow—until finally the Soviet Union itself collapsed, to be replaced by the Russian Republic.

That event bears all the marks of a transcendent mystery in history; unforeseen by all the prominent political analysts, it brought an end to the division between two worlds, the capitalist West and the socialist East. The Cold War came to an end. What followed was the Western capitalist process of globalization, surrounded by a new set of reductionisms.

Despite our valid criticisms of its economic and political effects, *globalization* is primarily an anthropological phenomenon that might better be called planetization. After living in dispersion in many regions of the world, humanity has begun to come together in one Common Home, the planet Earth. We have begun to see ourselves as a single species, with a common destiny.

Pierre Teilhard de Chardin foresaw this phenomenon in 1933, from his ecclesiastical exile in China. We are entering a new phase of human life, he said: the *noosphere*, a convergence of minds and hearts into a single common history, together with the history of the earth. This also represents an irruption of the Spirit, which is a Spirit of unity, reconciliation, and convergence in diversity.

The World Social Forums that began to take place in the year 2000 also reveal a unique irruption of the Spirit; we celebrate the

Spirit in the liturgy as *pater pauperum*, the father of the poor and defender of the humble. For the first time in modern history—in contrast with the gatherings of the rich in the city of Davos, Switzerland—the poor people of the world were able to bring together many thousands of people, first in Porto Alegre, Brazil, and then in other world cities, to share experiences of resistance and liberation, compare notes on creating microalternatives to the ruling system of domination, nourish their collective dream, and raise a powerful cry: another world is possible, another world is necessary.

In the World Social Forums that followed, at the regional and international level, we have seen the emergence of a new human paradigm, successfully organizing new modes of production, consumption, environmental conservation, and the inclusion of all humanity, beginning with the last and the least, in a shared project of guaranteeing life and hope for everyone. That is its importance: out of the depths of human despair has come a wisp of smoke, pointing to an inner fire that cannot be extinguished. In time it will become a blazing torch, illuminating a new way forward for humanity.

The Arab Spring that has set fire to all of northern Africa grew out of a search for freedom, respect for human rights, and the integration of women as equal players in the social process. Dictatorships were overthrown; democracies are being tested out; and religion is increasingly valued in society, apart from its fundamentalist aspects. These historic events must be interpreted, beyond their secular and social-political context, as manifestations of the Spirit of liberty and creativity.

We cannot deny that in a biblical and theological reading, the crisis of 2008 that shook the center of the world's economic and financial power—the great economic conglomerates that feed on the despair of the people—is also an irruption of the Holy Spirit. As we sing in the Church liturgy, the Spirit is "cleansing that which is unclean, watering that which is dry, healing that which is wounded." Is this catharsis and cleansing not the place to look for ways out of the crisis?

Even the movements led by victims of the economic and financial system in Europe, like the Indignados in Spain and England and Occupy Wall Street in the United States, reveal an energetic protest and a search for new forms of democracy and production—an energy and a search that, in the eyes of faith, must have been inspired by the Holy Spirit.

Ecological consciousness is growing in an increasing number of people around the world. The facts are undeniable: we have reached earth's limits, its ecosystems are being exhausted, and fossil fuel, the engine of all industrial processes, is nearly depleted. Extreme events come one after another: excessive heat in some places, freezing cold in others, the melting of the polar ice cap, the scarcity of water, the extinction of nearly a hundred thousand species every year (by 2013 data), desertification, deforestation, and a rate of global warming that may endanger the biosphere and all humanity in the next few decades; all these problems are questions of conscience. The Spirit is calling us to wake up and turn ourselves around.

We are primarily responsible for this ecological chaos. Unless we change the course of our economy, our politics, and our ethics, we may go the way of the dinosaurs. We urgently need a new paradigm of civilization, like those that have worked for other human cultures—the "good life in community" (*sumac kawsay*) of the Andean peoples; the "overall happiness index" of Bhutan; eco-socialism; a biocentric economy of solidarity; a "green economy" in the best sense of the word; projects focused on life, humanity, and a living earth, Gaia—all of which our economy, our politics, our culture, and our ethics were meant to serve.

The Fossilization of Religions and Churches

Religions and churches have always been the privileged setting for the experience of concrete, existential, ultimate meaning (the Meaning of all meaning), because they speak of infinite values. But religions and churches are not immune to the global crisis of our civilization. Certainly their nucleus has remained firm over time, but the language, rituals, doctrines, and discipline in which they express it have become fossilized. These institutions cling to the past, with no renewal in the transmission of their messages. They are still fountains—of dead water.

Sadly, the crisis has even penetrated the official institution of the Catholic Church. Instead of bravely facing the global crisis it has turned inward, taking refuge in past achievements, becoming a bastion of patriarchal, reactionary conservatism. Christian churches more than any other institution should dare to step up to the edge of heresy, because the Spirit is with them. They could propose solutions, open paths of renewal, and proclaim the newness around them, but instead they are held hostage by the monolithic ecclesiastical system and their assumed exclusivity. They attribute divine right to themselves, and are therefore untouchable. Moreover, they live on fear, suspicion, and condemnation. Yet we know that the opposite of faith is not atheism, but fear.

In recent decades the Catholic Church has been obsessively fearful of relativism. Its absolutism is as dangerous as the relativism it opposes: it calcifies history, enervates the creative drive, and betrays the Jesus tradition that was described by José Comblin in his monumental pneumatology. In the real world everything is relative—except God, hunger, and the suffering of the innocent, as Dom Pedro Casaldáliga says. The Church needs to find ways of being present in the world, in our own time, as a source of meaning and the joy of living. Most Christians seem so sad that one wonders if they have been redeemed, or if they believe in the resurrection of all flesh. Everyone has a right to hear the liberating message of Jesus, in ways that they can understand and experience. That right is denied them when we repeat catechetical doctrines from the past, recodified in the present without using methods of communication that work in this new age of information and the globalization of human life.

Everything seems to have changed with the arrival of a Pope from the new churches in the Third World, Pope Francis from

Argentina. He has energetically brought back the real tradition, which we call "the Jesus Tradition." It moves us toward a de-paganization of the Church, especially the styles historically adopted by cardinals and popes: the pagan habits of the Roman emperors, with their symbols of absolute imperial power and the pomp of Renaissance palaces and princely fashions.

Pope Francis, who likes to call himself the bishop of Rome, declined to wear a mozzetta, the richly embellished shawl worn by Roman emperors as a display of power. "The carnival is over," he said. Instead, he wore a simple white cape over his white robe, everyday shoes, and the black pants he has always worn.

But the true ecclesial revolution introduced by Pope Francis was his move to place Jesus, the poor, and real human beings—whether or not they call themselves believers—in the center of the Church.

The historical Jesus, not the triumphal Christ Pantocrator of later theology, has returned to the center of the Church. This Jesus, the Nazarene, brought a message centered on the image of a Father-God who also shows the traits of a mother: God's unconditional love, God's limitless mercy, God's nearness to the impoverished masses, and God's special concern for the humble and forgotten ones, to whom Jesus proclaimed the Reign of God. His words and gestures give them hope, endurance, and the ability to build a new, less evil society. He had the prophetic courage to denounce an economic-financial system that idolizes wealth and devours whole nations. Thus Jesus of Nazareth becomes a powerful ally of all who seek another, possible and necessary, world.

The poor have also returned to the center. In his first public interview, Pope Francis told the press: "How I long to see a poor Church, a Church for the poor." He was not speaking rhetorically, as popes have always done when they talk about an option for the poor without ever entering into direct contact with the poor. He was reaching out to the poorest of the poor, which in Europe means the immigrants from Africa and Eastern Europe. He visited them on the island of Lampedusa, in the refugee centers established by the Jesuits in Rome, and in Corsica, which has the highest rate of unemployment in all Italy.

He lives simply in the Residence of St. Martha, not in the pontifical palace; he eats in the dining hall with everyone else, and sleeps in one of the rooms for residents. He travels in an ordinary car, with only a small security detail, as we saw when he came to Brazil for the International Day of Youth. He shows how the Church can live in solidarity with the suffering people in the world. He has challenged religious orders not to use their monasteries and convents for profit-making events and businesses, but for hospitality to the poor, who are "the flesh of Christ."

Also at the center is the personal life of the concrete human person. Pope Francis sees the Church, not as a fortress to be defended from contamination by the world, but as an open house from which the ministers can reach out to the faithful, invite them in, and make them feel at home. He is in dialogue with everyone. He talked personally with a great Italian journalist, Eugenio Scalfari, a nonbeliever, about the relationship between faith, science, and unbelief.

These words, from a long interview with the Jesuit journal *La Civiltà Cattolica* in late September 2013, reveal his vision of the Church and its mission in the world:

> I see more and more clearly that what the Church most needs today is the ability to heal the wounds and warm the hearts of the faithful, from up close. I see the Church as a field hospital after a battle. It does no good to ask an injured soldier if he has high cholesterol or blood sugar. First we have to cure the wounds; later we can ask about the rest. We have to start at the bottom. The Church sometimes focuses on little things, petty precepts. First we have to tell people, "Jesus has saved you." Therefore the ministers of the Church should be, above all, ministers of mercy. People need us to walk with them; their wounds need to be cured.

The ministers of the Church should be merciful, should care about human persons, should accompany them as the good Samaritan did, washing, cleansing, and lifting up his neighbor. This is the pure Gospel. God is greater than sin. Structural and organizational reforms are secondary, they come later; the first is a change of attitude. Ministers of the Gospel must be able to warm the hearts of human persons, walk with them at night, enter into dialogue and even go into the night with them, into their darkness, without getting lost. The People of God are looking for pastors, not for administrators or government clerks.

The quotation is long, but it shows his understanding of the Church and its liberating mission in today's world. Pope Francis represents a springtime of the Church, bringing Christian joy and hope to the world.

One problem remains unresolved in the institutional revolution introduced by Pope Francis: the tension between charism and power. Power evolved in the Church, because the community had to organize and ensure its continuity in history. This has been called the Petrine moment (after St. Peter, guarantor of the apostolic tradition). But as we said before, this power became monarchical and absolutistic, concentrated in the hands of a minority of Christians: the clergy, with the Pope at its head. This unequal structure, which goes against the explicit instructions of Jesus, led to a fictitious unity expressed in the unconditional submission of everyone else; that in turn has produced infantile Christians, lacking in creativity and authenticity. Despite the fact that according to St. Paul the Spirit is given to all, that its charisms are shared by the will of the Spirit and not subject to hierarchical approval, the new ecclesiastical structure has eliminated the Holy Spirit from common doctrine.

In other words, the Pauline moment was lost (after St. Paul, the prince of Christian freedom). But the Church is based on both apostles, Peter and Paul. To exclude or restrict one of them means deforming the Church, against the Jesus tradition. It is important to remember that wherever power prevails—even in the realm of the sacred—love, compassion, and creativity disappear. It is in the nature of power to use force, to ally itself with other powers and subject to its control whatever threatens or opposes its power. Charismatic leaders, reformers, and innovators throughout history have been persecuted, condemned, or eliminated by the powerful.

The institution of the Inquisition (whatever new name we give it) has always been the great instrument for controlling, repressing, and condemning any potential threat to established power. It is perhaps the greatest obstacle to evangelization and dialogue, because it values order more than life, discipline more than creativity, self-righteousness more than openness to others.

"Do not quench the Spirit," Paul warned (1 Thessalonians 5:19). But in recent centuries the Spirit has often been quenched by institutional power, which has never been able to maintain a creative tension between two legitimate poles: power and charism. This was the theme of my book *Church: Charism and Power*, which was criticized by the successors of the Inquisition. Note that the subtitle was not "Charism *or* Power," but "Charism *and* Power." We need power to ensure the perpetuation of Jesus' message in history. And we need charism to uphold power in its servant role, so that the Jesus Tradition does not become fossilized in doctrines, rites, and canonical norms. The purpose of charism is to continually refresh and renew the message in the face of historical mutations. Unless we hold these two energies together, we lose the complex, dialectical balance of order and creativity that a healthy community needs. Without this articulation of the two poles, power leads to neglect of the Spirit—as often happened in the Latin Church, where the sacred power of the hierarchy gained hegemony and ended up subduing the manifestations of the Spirit.

The great German theologian J. A. Möhler (1838) used to say in an ironic tone: "God created the hierarchy, and thus generously gave us everything we need until the end of time." That wry comment later became a traditional teaching, explicitly affirmed by Popes Gregory XVI (1846) and Pius X (1914): "The Church is an unequal, hierarchical, and perfect society: on the one hand a hierarchy that teaches and commands, and on the other the faithful, who hear and obey." According to this teaching, the division between clergy and laity is established by divine right, and therefore cannot be changed. This view of power soon leads to hierarchies, discriminations, and inequalities that neglect the Spirit and its gifts, or create obstacles to its action. This is where the Catholic Charismatic Renewal (CCR) becomes important; it can strengthen the practice of charism, and it can (or should) challenge power to fulfill its role of service rather than domination.

In our time the place of the Holy Spirit is being taken over not only by the hierarchy, but by the Universal Catechism of the Catholic Church, published during the pontificate of John Paul II. As José Comblin has rightly observed: "The Universal Catechism places everything on the same level, and allows no further investigation. It imposes a single interpretation on every continent and every culture. All cultures must understand revelation as it is understood in Rome. This interpretation inevitably remains abstract, unaffected by the light of the historical situation; that is, it is in danger of becoming irrelevant. The publication of this Catechism makes the action of the Holy Spirit redundant. Nothing is left for the Spirit to do, since the Catechism explains everything for everyone" (*O Espíritu Santo*, 116).

Apart from this inflation of sacred power, which leaves little room for the Holy Spirit, we should also be concerned with the disease of fundamentalism that is weakening almost all the religions and churches. We see it in their increased claims to exclusivity, as the only bearer of truth and the only way to God. Fundamentalism, in political parties or in religions and churches, always leads to violence and to structures of exclusion. It tears apart the unity of the human fabric, and the work of the Spirit in every people and every heart. The Spirit always arrives ahead of the preacher;

wherever there is love, forgiveness, mercy, and brotherhood, the Spirit is there with its gifts. And we know beyond doubt that those gifts are present in every people and every culture.

One emerging answer to fundamentalism is "experientialism," which embraces all kinds of experience. Experience is a phenomenon of human subjectivity, rich and fruitful, which deserves encouragement and respect. The Spirit comes through sensations and perceptions of the sacred, but if it is not accompanied by discernment, subjectivity can easily become subjectivism; in that case experience never reaches out to other subjectivities, looking for common ground with them. Subjectivism opens the way to exotic beliefs like astrology, divination according to the *I Ching*, superficial shamanism, and other magical practices. It looks to uncontrollable, suprahuman powers for solutions to the human drama, solutions that do not require any personal commitment from the human being.

This has given rise to all sorts of spiritual experiences from the Orient, from indigenous cultures, and from the Celtic and other ancient traditions. It offers a mystical-spiritual pastiche that only increases human alienation, instead of suggesting autonomous paths to self-realization based on creativity and freedom. Here the charismatic character of the Spirit is transmuted into a psychic character, distorting the essence of humanity. St. Paul was right to distinguish between the *psychicói* (psychic phenomena) and *pneumatikói* (the bearers of *Pneuma*).

Self-help literature, promoted by gurus and spiritual coaches, offers another widely popular way out. This genre—built out of fragments of spiritual and religious traditions, depth psychology, and some elements of the new cosmology and communications theory—gives its adherents the illusion of an easy path to happiness, immediate success, and inner peace. It is deceptive because instead of addressing the real, fragile, and contradictory human condition, it offers placebos; the reader moves hopelessly from one self-help book to another in an endless search for remedies. It does not require us to face the contradictory challenges of human life directly, by building our own inner synthesis: struggling with our demons and angels in order to establish a viable relationship with the world, with nature, with other people, with ourselves, and with the Ultimate Reality, which is the only basis of true peace.

The Irrationality of Modern Reason

Modernity is based on in-depth analytical reason, which led to the creation of modern science based on physics and mathematics. Everything became an object of knowledge, which made it possible to change reality. The earth was reduced to its physical-chemical-ecological substance, its goods and services to be exploited through the processes of industrialization. This kind of reason was used by the political powers as a tool for the domination of other, technically less advanced, peoples and cultures in Africa, Latin America, and the rest of the world. It facilitated the colonization and subjection of nations, whose natural wealth was made to serve the interests of the European powers. Their goal is progress, understood as unlimited material growth, the true obsession of modernity. Growth is falsely identified as development; in contrast, real development would promote human life in its many dimensions, especially in the free choice of lifestyles and goals.

This obsession with growth leads to a desire for wealth without humanitarian or ethical limits, destroying nature and generating enormous social inequality, which in turn leads to injustice at the planetary level. The current ecological crisis, as seen in global warming and the depletion of the small planet's limited resources, is approaching its final paroxysm: a limited earth cannot withstand unlimited exploitation. The living Gaia must eventually react, and defend itself however it can. But after so much exploitation it has lost much of its ability to restore what has been taken away from it. In other words, earth is becoming unsustainable. Unless we change our behavior, the consequence may well be social and ecological disaster.

This behavior has become a paradigm for our rationalistic, objectivistic, materialistic, and utilitarian civilization, which has lost its sense of wholeness, fragmenting reality in order to understand

and control it more effectively. Such a paradigm leaves little room for the Spirit, or for spirituality. Rather it shows reason run wild, absolutizing itself and holding itself up as the only criterion of validity and social acceptance. Here we see the irrationality of reason, which as we have said, has created the means for exterminating humanity itself and deeply wounding the biosphere. "Smart" violence against human communities has wiped out many of the indigenous cultures of Latin America, led to destructive wars, and produced the Shoah, the mass murder of Jews, Roma, and disabled people. Today we possess enough chemical, biological, and nuclear weapons to destroy the whole human species many times over. This kind of reason is irrational, brutal, and hostile to life.

Reason ran wild when it made itself absolute, systematically repressing the emotional, affective, relational side of human intelligence. Emotions were said to interfere with the objectivity of knowledge, but since then the new sciences, beginning with quantum physics and cosmology, have discovered that all knowledge is entangled with feelings and other elements of personal and social subjectivity.

The roots of reason are interwoven with human subjectivity, through the limbic system which first appeared in mammalian evolution over two hundred million years ago. Mammals brought something new to the face of the earth: affect, care for others, and love. We humans are affective mammals. At the deepest level we have a capacity to feel, to care, and to love. Our whole structure of values and ethics is built on that foundation.

Reason came later, some seven million years ago, when the neocortical brain began to grow along with the limbic brain. The neocortex enables us to develop concepts, rational orders, and worldviews. Above analytical reason is the intelligence of intuition and contemplation, which we recognize as wisdom. Analytical reason lies midway between the most ancient and the most recent levels.

We need analytical reason in order to manage our world and attend to our needs, but today it needs to be enriched by relational and affective reason. Relational reason makes us aware of the gravity of the present crisis; it enables us to hear the suffering of the poor and the cry of the oppressed earth. Relational reason, rooted in the heart, leads us to embrace the earth as our Mother; it also awakens compassion for all who suffer for, care for, and love everything that exists and lives.

Through spirituality, the Spirit makes reason whole. It enlightens reason for the service of life, rather than profit, and awakens the positive senses that can turn us away from the abyss we are now reaching.

The Contribution of World Feminism

The French philosopher of science Gaston Bachelard and the Russian theologian Evdokimov were ahead of their time in noticing the sexist bias of modern science. That bias comes from an overemphasis on the dimension of *animus*, reflecting power and the will to dominate, and the repression of *anima*, reflecting affect, feeling, and spirituality in relation to vital processes. The most important contribution to this discussion, however, has come from feminism and ecofeminism. Women have not only denounced male domination as a gender issue, but have gone on to challenge our whole patriarchal culture.

It was feminism that drew attention to the two energies that make up the human identity, which were so well described by C. G. Jung: *anima* and *animus*. Both are present and active in all human beings. However, women are the privileged (though not the only) bearers of *anima*, the dimension in both men and women that accounts for sensitivity, cooperation, the ability to decode the messages of reality, and the dimension of worship and spirituality.

The rise of women in all spheres of human activity—their role in the world of labor, knowledge, politics, and the arts, but especially in their reflections on the condition of women—has to be seen as a powerful irruption of the Spirit in history.

We urgently need the feminine dimensions women bring to light in order to overcome today's global crisis. All life is in danger. Woman is at the heart of life, for she gives life and cares for it through all time. Now more than ever she has a messianic, salvific mission. As we shall see, it was through a woman, Mary, that the Spirit was embodied in history. The Spirit has a special affinity with women; in the Middle Eastern languages, "spirit" is a feminine noun.

The twenty-first century will be the age of women; through the failure of men with their arrogance and dehumanizing power, as we see in most countries, women have been assuming an increasing degree of collective responsibility. They will make it possible to overcome the crisis through the irruption of a new paradigm, centered on the fundamental values that women live by and witness to: life, humanity, and the earth. These are the pillars on which another civilizing enterprise can be built, oriented to care, cooperation, solidarity with the last and the least, compassion for those who suffer in society and in nature, and love as the force of cohesion and fulfillment of human happiness.

Catholic Charismatic Renewal

A Mission for the Renewal of Community

We have seen how the Church of Liberation drew out the liberating implications of the Christian message, leading the churches to take the side of the victims, creating new forms of pastoral action and a new way of being Church, highlighting practices of transformation and liberation through the Christian Base Communities and social ministries. Catholic Charismatic Renewal (CCR) complements this experience with a much-needed emphasis on prayer and spirituality, based on the work of the Spirit in human beings and in the world. We experience its power through the spiritualization of Christian life at the personal and community level.

To contrast the Church of Liberation with the Charismatic Church would imply a biased, reductionist perspective. They are both born of the same Spirit, which enables the transformation of both the inner and the outer world.

Our prayer "Come, Holy Spirit, come soon" has been heard. Along with the Church of Liberation, the Spirit has given rise to the Catholic Charismatic Renewal. We must note, however, that this irruption began more than two centuries ago, when the Protestant churches felt the "awakening of the Spirit" and the "baptism of the Holy Spirit."

The role of John Wesley (1703–1791), founder of the Methodist Movement, is especially worth remembering. He was the son of an Anglican minister and became an Anglican priest himself. In 1738, reacting against the rigidity of his church, he decided to become an itinerant preacher and to encourage others to become lay preachers, especially laborers who were exploited by early capitalism. He saw Christianity as a living encounter with God. Wesley talked about "the religion of the heart," which he described simply as "justice, peace, and joy in the Holy Spirit." These realities are not meant to be thought about, but felt in one's life; otherwise Christianity becomes something dead (see A. Corten 1995, 56). Wesley's Methodism began to spread across Great Britain in 1729, and later reached northern Europe, the United States, Africa, and finally Latin America.

Charismatic Renewal first emerged in Protestant communities in 1956, in the Catholic Church at Duquesne University in 1966, and a year later at Notre Dame University in South Bend, Indiana. There it began with a weekend retreat from February 17 to 19, 1967, when a group of students and professors set out to live the spirit of Pentecost. The Church was born at Pentecost, and this new Pentecost would give rise to the renewal of the Church.

I emphasized the importance of the Spirit in my doctoral thesis, presented at the University of Munich in 1968 and published under the guidance of the theologian Joseph Ratzinger: *The Church as Sacrament of the Experience of the World.* Two long chapters are devoted to the Holy Spirit as a force in ecclesial organization, based not on *potestas sacra* but on the multiplicity and simultaneity of charisms, especially the charism of leadership and unity-building.

Pope Leo XIII had already anticipated the importance of the Spirit in his encyclical *Divinum illud munus*, published on May 9, 1897. He lamented the neglect of the Spirit by the faithful and by the Church itself, and called on them to worship it more faithfully. But it was Pope John XXIII who most eagerly anticipated the coming of the Spirit, in his convocation of the Second Vatican Council on December 25, 1961; there he spoke of "a new Pentecost" for the Church. Echoing this call, Paul VI said at an audience on November 20, 1972, that the Church was in need of "a perpetual Pentecost." John Paul II also devoted an encyclical to the Spirit, *Dominum et vivificantem*, in 1986.

I shall not undertake a detailed history of the birth and development of CCR here. I only want to put it in context as an expression of the coming of the Holy Spirit and note its contribution to the renewal of the Church.

As I said earlier, at times of great crisis the Spirit comes down in the midst of the turbulence, to bring order and to awaken creative minds. Our world society has been marked by the savage massification of peoples and the destruction of cultural identities. Personal subjectivity is overwhelmed by the entertainment industry and the marketing of products. Bureaucratic regulation and controls have made the life of societies altogether too artificial. The prevailing style in the Catholic Church even after *aggiornamento*, and in the mainline Protestant churches, is still doctrinal, ritualistic, and excessively cerebral, leaving little room for bodily expression and creativity.

In this context the Spirit has irrupted in prayer groups, through free bodily expression and spontaneous words and prayers, without control by the clergy.

It began in Brazil in 1969 with the participation of two North American Jesuits, Fr. Harold Rahm and Fr. Edward Dougherty, in retreats held in the city of Campinas. From there it spread across Brazil like wildfire, first under the leadership of priests familiar with the movement in the United States, and then independently. Fr. Harold's book, *Seréis batizados no Espírito*, became a theoretical and practical guidebook for the communities of prayer. The First National Encounter of Charismatic Renewal was held in Campinas in 1973.

The CCR gained momentum with the Canção Nova (New Song) Community, under the leadership of the conservative-leaning Fr. Jonás Abib de Cachoeira Paulista. His followers reached thousands of believers through their own television channel, sometimes engaging polemically with other Pentecostal and evangelical groups, and sometimes with liberation theology.

There are over fifteen million followers of CCR in Brazil, of whom about 70 percent are women. Most of its social base consists of believers from the middle class. People in this group are often under pressure from the dominant consumer culture, which weakens social relationships, generating anxiety, fear, and a painful existential emptiness. This leads to a search for meaning, to which CCR is responding effectively. But it is also spreading in low-income urban neighborhoods and in other economically poor sectors.

Several characteristics of CCR are (1) the centrality of the Holy Spirit in its charisms, gifts, and fruits; (2) "baptism in the Spirit," expressed as inward conversion and total openness to the inspiration of the Holy Spirit; (3) the mutual laying on of hands as a way of invoking the Holy Spirit; (4) love for Jesus Christ and Mary, the principal bearers of the Spirit; (5) the practice of personal and community prayer; (6) meditative reading of the scriptures; (7) frequent participation in the Eucharist; (8) emphasis on God's praise; (9) speaking in tongues (glossolalia); (10) brotherly love; and (11) an unconditional acceptance of Church doctrine, with obedience and devotion to the hierarchy.

CCR sought to assure its place in the official Church by seeking approval from the doctrinal authorities of the Vatican. Their statute—the International Service of Charismatic Renewal—was adopted on September 14, 1993, by a decree of the Pontifical Council for the Laity.

CCR now has over a hundred million participants around the world. It represents a new face of the Church. Instead of emphasizing the cross and the strict rule of traditional piety, it introduced the joy of the Spirit, spontaneous expressiveness, creative prayer, and beautiful hymns. Its liturgies are marked by intimacy with God and celebration of the life of faith, rather than ritualization. It has helped overcome the formality, rigidity, and inertia of official religious conventions and celebrations, by enriching their symbols and participation.

One of its greatest contributions to the life of faith has been the retrieval of emotional intelligence and sensitive, relational reason, which had fallen into disrepute with the crisis of functional-analytical reason (see L. Boff, *El cuidado esencial*, 1999, and *El cuidado necesario*, 2012). As we know from anthropology and other sciences, the deepest dimension of humanity is not found in *logos* (rationality), but in *pathos* (affect). Human beings are made up of feelings, passions, and "oceanic" experiences, along with their ability to understand and explain things.

Our sense of reason, always important but never exclusively so, grows out of this ability. Reason is interwoven with feelings, interests, and values. The proper place of religion, spirituality, and ethics is not in reason but in affect, in the ability to feel in depth and in totality. By emphasizing the experience of the Spirit in the life of the Church, CCR has restored this forgotten dimension, so necessary for the humanization of our relationships with God and nature.

The consolidation of CCR may help the Church enter a new age, if it is broadened to include other elements of the Jesus Tradition. Charismatic renewal and the Church of Liberation can be the two lungs of the Christian community: one through life and intimacy with God in the power of the Holy Spirit; the other through following Christ and bearing a living, Spirit-filled witness to the liberating action of Christians amid the suffering of human beings and the devastation of the natural world. Both ways of being Church come from the same source: from the Spirit and from following Jesus, who died and is risen.

But everything healthy can also become sick. There are reductionist tendencies in the overall tone of the CCR movement. Some important elements of the Christian message are lost; without them Jesus' legacy is diminished and becomes less effective. For example, the movement is not always sensitive to the drama of the world and the tragic fate of the poor. That is, the issue of social and ecological justice at the global level seldom appears as a theme of reflection and practice.

Spiritual experience, which is so important to CCR, leaves little room for theological reflection and critique; few of the outstanding names in theology are associated with CCR. One exception is the German theologian Heribert Mühlen, with his very scholarly book *Renovación de la fe Cristiana: Charisma, espíritu, liberación* (1974) and his two-volume *Iniciación a la experiencia cristiana fundamental* (1976).

A vague fundamentalism prevails in the charismatic interpretation of biblical texts. It is easy to claim healings and interventions of the Spirit, without the discernment that comes from analysis with the currently available resources of critical theology, the human sciences, and deep reality (cf. S. Carrillo Alday, *A renovação no Espíritu Santo*, 1986).

We must remember that in the early Church, Pentecost was the point of departure and not the end point. The outpouring of the Holy Spirit in tongues of fire was the beginning of the Church's mission, and it has not yet ended. The power of evil never comes to an end; it has to be confronted by the power of good, which is the Spirit. Pentecost is always an ongoing process. That is why we pray "Come, Holy Spirit," and "Renew the face of the earth."

The evangelization carried out by CCR needs to be enriched by a social dimension that implies concern for the poor, who are best understood as impoverished and oppressed by unjust social relations, and the renewal of society as it is clearly envisioned in the liturgical Sequence of the Feast of Pentecost. Bearing in mind that in the best ecumenical exegesis of the Lord's Prayer is a synthesis of Jesus' message in the form of a prayer; we can clearly see it in two dimensions. The first part expresses praise for *our Father* in heaven and prays for the coming of God's Kingdom. In the second part we pray for *our daily bread*, and for the reconciliation of our broken society. We should never separate what Jesus held together: Our Father and our daily bread. Jesus' passion for God, whom he revealed as *Abba*, should always go hand in hand with his passion for those who need bread and reconciliation.

CCR rightly emphasizes the dimension of our Father; it rejoices in this revelation, by singing and dancing with God's sons and daughters in the feast of the Spirit. But it gives insufficient attention to the bread for which so many people cry out in hunger; hunger cannot wait. To make its evangelization complete, CCR should embody this essential dimension of Jesus' legacy: sharing bread and relieving hunger.

This is where the theology of liberation, purified of its own reductionism, can helpfully share its thinking and practice with respect to *our daily bread*—which is not truly ours unless it is made and eaten collectively. CCR can help the theology of liberation remember that our commitment is to *our Father* and the Kingdom. Together the theology of liberation and CCR can achieve wholeness and offer all humanity a convincing, integral evangelization.

A Mission to Evangelize the Hierarchical Church?

But there is another mission that the Catholic Charismatic Renewal should undertake more intentionally, although it seems not to have recognized it yet: helping the hierarchical Church overcome the systemic crisis that has plagued it since the early centuries. As we discussed earlier, there has been an unfortunate separation between the clergy and laity. Power was left in the hands of the hierarchy, with no lay participation in its decision making.

That trend took shape and gained momentum with Pope Leo I (440–461). A great lawyer and statesman, he copied the absolutist and authoritarian power of the Roman emperor. He applied a purely juridical, rather than pastoral, interpretation to three New Testament texts about Peter: Peter as the rock on which the Church would be built (Matthew 16:18), as the one charged with strengthening his brothers' faith (Luke 22:32), and as the shepherd called to feed Jesus' sheep (John 21:15). The biblical and jesuanic meaning of those texts is directly contrary to their juridical meaning; Jesus was talking about love, service, and the renunciation of all supremacy.

But the absolutist reading from Roman law prevailed. Leo I assumed the title of Supreme Pontiff and Pope, which until then had been reserved exclusively to Roman emperors. Other popes later began to use purple robes, miters, golden thrones, staffs, stoles, cloaks, capes, and other imperial accessories; they also built palaces and introduced courtly manners that are still practiced by today's cardinals and bishops.

These styles are a scandal to many Christians, who know from the Gospels that Jesus was a poor and humble laborer. It has become increasingly clear that the hierarchy is closer to Herod's palace than to the stable of Bethlehem.

But one thing is especially hard to understand: in their zeal to legitimize this transformation and guarantee the absolute power of the Pope, they issued a series of forged documents. Among these are the "Donation of Constantine," written in France in the sixteenth century, and the "Pseudo-Isidorian Decretals," later incorporated in the Code of Gratian (the first great codification of canon law), which strengthened the centralized power of Rome for centuries. Cardinal Nicholas of Cusa in the sixteenth century was the first to prove the forgery of the decretals. But these documents were used against rival princes to justify the centralized, monarchical, and absolutist "Roman system."

The power of the popes kept on growing. Gregory VII († 1085) proclaimed himself the absolute ruler of the Church and the world in his *Dictatus Papae* ("the dictatorship of the Pope," 1075); Innocent III († 1216) declared himself the vicar-representative of Christ, and finally, Innocent IV († 1254) took the role of representative of God. With that authority, under Pius IX in 1870, the Pope was declared infallible on matters of doctrine and morality.

Curiously, the hierarchical Church never retracted or corrected these excesses, which have served it well. They remain in force, to the shame of those who still believe in the poor Nazarene, the humble artisan and Mediterranean peasant, who was persecuted, executed on the cross, and raised in order to resist everyone— even in the Church—who seeks power and more power. The hierarchical view of the Church unforgivably fails to recognize that according to the Gospel (Matthew 25:45), the true vicars of Christ are the poor, the hungry, and the thirsty.

Here is an opportunity for the CCR to offer a prophetic criticism, speaking with clarity and not anger, out of love for a Church increasingly faithful to Jesus' legacy and open to the moving of the Spirit. The Spirit is asking the Church to renounce power for the sake of service, to give up its palatial apparatus in favor of simplicity and transparency.

Certainly this model of Church, with the hierarchy on one side and the laity on the other, is now being strongly criticized by theologians, biblical scholars, the ecumenical movement, and advocates of global democracy for its great distance from the Jesus Tradition. The Church is in a deep and widespread crisis. Unless it undergoes a transformation—along the evangelical lines foreseen by the Second Vatican Council, never fully implemented, but now brought back by Pope Francis—the crisis of the hierarchical Church will deepen, perhaps irreversibly.

The balance between charism and power has been broken, in favor of power. This power controls, subdues, and sometimes suffocates charism. It is not surprising that authorities in both the Vatican and the National Conference of Bishops of Brazil (CNBB) have taken care to establish limits and subject the charisma of the CCR to the criteria of ecclesiastical power. Pope John Paul II did so on November 23, 1980, when he admonished the CCR for its possible excesses. In 1994 the CNBB published a set of "Pastoral Guidelines on Catholic Charismatic Renewal" (CNBB document #53).

Here again we see the temptation of institutional power to place limits on charism and weaken its transformative potential.

The limits are strict. In both documents we can see the hierarchical power diminishing the nature of charism. As often happens in the Latin tradition, it does not respect the role of the Spirit, which is to create something new, to be the historical embodiment of God's dream of continually transforming Jesus' message into good news.

This is where the CCR's mission comes in. It must see the future not merely as a continuation of the past and present. Its mission would be to evangelize the hierarchical Church to use its services, gifts, and charisms to serve and inspire the community. The hierarchy claims to evangelize the world, but who will evangelize the hierarchy? Who will set limits on its greed for power, which as we know, is the source of intrigue, ambition, and the quest for privilege and prestige? And which incidentally leads to reprimands, reassignments, and canonical penalties.

The Holy Spirit has not only inspired CCR to renew the spiritual life of the world. Its greater mission, not yet fully recognized and accepted, should be to live by the charism of prophecy: gently and energetically to point out the excesses of sacred power—pedophilia and financial scandals are among the expressions of power without charism—and suggest creative methods of leadership and motivation to service, following the example of Jesus and the Apostles. This mission must be nourished by love, the supreme gift of the Spirit, mutual caring, and mercy for those who suffer. What Jesus asks of us is not hierarchy (the power to command) but *hierodulia* (service to others).

If the CCR does not take on this urgent, challenging mission, who will? It may suffer insults, misunderstandings, and even persecution. These will have to be faced in the spirit of the beatitudes, with the gifts of courage, endurance, resilience, and patience, which are always promised to the faithful.

In conclusion: the irruption of the Holy Spirit in this new, planetary age—to make the Catholic Church and other churches more spiritual, more evangelical, more faithful in following the poor and humble Jesus, and especially more ecologically conscious in order to protect human life on this planet and the future of our salvation—is a heavenly gift that we must accept with open and grateful hearts. We are living in what may be the end times. According to the scriptures, that is when the Spirit will come upon all flesh.

It comes in response to our cry: "Come, Holy Spirit." "Come to renew the face of the earth." "Come soon, come urgently!"

2

In the Beginning Was the Spirit

A New Way of Thinking about God

In this long introduction we have called on the Holy Spirit to come quickly. Now, even before we can fully engage in theological reflection on the Holy Spirit, we need to deepen our understanding of the word "spirit." That word has become almost meaningless in today's world, both in literature and in popular culture.

Recovering the Word "Spirit"

In today's educated culture, "spirit" is the opposite of matter. We know more or less what matter is; we can measure it, weigh it, manipulate and change it. By contrast, spirit is intangible, undefined, and even nebulous. Matter is the source of material values, which have been central to human experience in recent centuries. Modern science is all about the investigation and control of matter. It explores the deepest reaches of material reality: subatomic particles, the Higgs Field where the first condensation of energy took place, hadrons, and the elusive "God particle."

Einstein showed that matter and energy are one and the same. Matter does not exist in itself; it is energy, concentrated in a rich field of interactions. Theology has not begun to take seriously the meaning of this way of understanding reality; theology is still a primarily materialist, substantialist discipline.

The state sees itself as the organizer of material production by means of human labor, technology, and small and large enterprise in order to meet human needs through market capitalism and the accumulation of wealth. But the state is also responsible for overseeing intangible values such as transparency, cooperation, respect for differences of culture and gender, and the ecological and social health of the environment. These dimensions are also related to the spiritual dimensions of existence.

Spiritual values, in the accepted modern sense, are part of the superstructure and have no place in our scientific categories. They belong to the world of subjectivity, to be overseen by individuals or by religious groups. José Comblin is not exaggerating when he says: "When someone speaks of 'spiritual values,' everyone thinks it is a businessman at an elegant, lavish Rotary or Lion's Club dinner washed down with fine wine. For most people, 'spiritual values' are eloquent but empty words" (*O Espíritu no mundo*, 9). Or else they belong to the vocabulary of moralized, spiritualized ecclesiastical discourse, which has nothing kind to say about the modern world.

This is why we usually hear the expression "spiritual values" from conservative-leaning clergy, talking about the specific role of the Church in society: that is, to protect and promote "spiritual goods," which are generally equivalent to "moral values." They often describe the crisis of today's world in terms of its neglect of the spiritual world, rather than distortions in the political, economic, or environmental field. And they understand "the neglect of the spiritual" as failure to attend religious celebrations or to talk directly about religion.

But the official discourse of "spiritual values" has lost its legitimacy with the recent scandals of pedophile priests, first concealed by the Vatican hierarchy but finally recognized as crimes and brought to the civil courts, and with the financial scandals associated with the Vatican Bank. Spiritual values are still important, but the official institution proclaiming them sounds like a voice in the desert; most people are no longer listening.

The word "spirit" means a great deal in popular culture. It conveys a certain magical conception of the world, in contrast to the rationality people learn at school. For many people, especially in the indigenous and Afro-Brazilian cultures, the world is inhabited by good and evil spirits that act on reality and affect such life situations as health, illness, intimate relationships, success and failure, good and bad luck. Spiritism describes this view of the world in terms of reincarnation: the soul is reincarnated to be purified, to grow, and after a long cleansing, to reach God. This belief is more widespread than we realize, not only in the popular sectors but at all levels of society; some of its adherents are highly educated, and some are Christians, including members of the Catholic Church.

In recent years there has been a surprising loss of enthusiasm for the material world and its promises, which are now recognized as false. The overemphasis on rationality in every sphere of life and the rampant growth of consumerism have generated existential saturation and disillusionment. Happiness is not to be found in material things, but in the domain of the heart: affect, love, solidarity, and compassion.

People everywhere are looking for new spiritual experiences, that is, feelings that go beyond immediate self-interest and the day-to-day struggle for life. These feelings bring a new perspective of light and hope into the marketplace of ideas and conventional answers, offered by the communications media and by "institutions of meaning" such as religions, churches, and philosophies. They draw strength from television and from massive religious spectacles, which by their very nature undermine the reverent and sacred aspect of all true religion. In a market society, religion and spirituality have also become commodities available for general consumption.

Despite the marketization of the religious world there is growing interest in spirituality, although it usually takes the form of exoticism, mysticism, and even the literature of self-help. Cracks are developing in the banality of the world and the grayness of mass society. Movements are arising in the Christian world, revolving around the Holy Spirit. Pentecostal churches and char-ismatic movements are focusing on the third article of the Creed: "I believe in the Holy Spirit." After centuries in the "Age of the Son," are we perhaps, as some people believe, moving into a new and longed-for "Age of the Holy Spirit"?

These changes suggest a retrieval of the positive, even antiestab-lishment, meaning of the word "spirit." It is a hopeful meaning, no longer diminished by the modernist suspicion of everything that is not filtered through the screen of reason. Reason does not have all the answers. Some things are irrational; some are arational. In every human being there is a world of passion, affect, and sincere feelings, expressed through relational and emotional intelligence. The spirit is not opposed to reason. The spirit needs reason but goes beyond it, carrying it to a higher level of intelligence, contemplation, and a higher sense of life and history.

Spirit-Laden Realities

Let us look at some experiences of life and spirit that can help us better understand the reality of the Spirit of God.

The Power of Nature, Howling and Trembling

Scene one: We hear the distant rumble of rain falling on the dense Amazon jungle, like a fierce animal shaking itself in the wind. The dark sky roars. The enormous blossoms shudder. The branches wail, rubbing against each other. Then the rain comes in a loud rush, as if someone had opened the floodgates of heaven. A deaf, terrifying fear invades the soul. There is nowhere to run.

Suddenly we realize that we are shaking, howling, weeping, and wailing with everything around us. Then, slowly, everything stops, and a tenuous mist rises from the drenched soil. Nature comes alive; it has been renewed with all its pulsating majesty. We have experienced something of what I call the spirit as movement, life, a whirlwind.

Scene two: The *sertão* of northeastern Brazil is dry and barren. Here and there one sees animal bones bleached by the dog-day sun. Only a few cacti keep watch over the parched landscape. In the distance a reddish cloud emerges and grows larger. A soft breeze begins to blow, sending dust devils scudding across the ground. The breeze becomes a wind. The cacti bend like ghosts. The wind blows harder, whistling across the rocks. Now it is a squall, and then a powerful storm.

The dry bones blow around and gather in mounds. A red dust cloud covers the horizon. Thunder crashes; fierce lightning slices across the sky. Heavy raindrops begin to pelt the ground. Suddenly they become a flood, crashing noisily down on the wounded land. The whirling wind forms a moving wave and disappears into a patch of *caatinga* bushes.

This is the pain-racked *sertão*, gasping for breath. After a little while, and another little while, we hear the rain falling eagerly on the thirsty ground. After a day, and another day, delicate green shoots begin pushing up everywhere. The gentle breeze is like the breathing of a child who lies satisfied on his mother's breast.

The spirit is like the breathing of nature, a wellspring of life, the power that turns the dry *caatinga* patches of the northeastern *sertão* into a copious garden.

Life as an Expression of the Spirit

Life is always a mystery, although we can describe the complex conditions in which it emerges.

Ilya Prigogine, winner of a Nobel Prize for his work in thermodynamics, has shown that life was born when the elements reached a high degree of complexity and disequilibrium. It came about as a way of overcoming chaos (*Order Out of Chaos*, 1984), establishing a new dynamic equilibrium. Christian de Duve, a Nobel laureate in medicine, added that at a certain high level of complexity, life emerges as a cosmic imperative everywhere in the universe (*Vital Dust*, 1996).

But science also recognizes the mysterious character of life (Schröder, De Duve, Capra). We can describe the conditions in which it emerges, but we have no idea what it really is. Finally we realize that we cannot define life; we can only live it, defend it, embrace it, locate ourselves within it. We only experience life and understand it by living it fully.

Life begins with an organism, a composite of many factors and elements revolving around a center. An organism is complex matter, but it is also something else entirely; it is laden with information (the genetic code) that has none of the characteristics of matter. Matter and energy are always interacting with their surroundings, self-regulating and self-creating.

Biologists talk endlessly about the unique and mysterious character of life. It is an evolutionary emergence, the supreme outcome of the cosmic process. For instance, bacteria—the most primitive life forms, which evolved 3.8 billion years ago—display the same intrinsic vitality they had then. They do not lose their structure even at temperatures close to absolute zero (−273° Celsius); rather they keep their vitality, regardless of the passage of time. They can recover all their functions, even after many thousands of years frozen in deep ice. Bacteria, frozen in the hide of a mammoth ten thousand years ago in Siberia, revived when they were brought back to normal temperatures. Other bacteria have been found after millions of years in deposits of mineral salts; they too returned to life and began to reproduce as they had before.

We know that viruses, bacteria, algae, and protozoa are, in a certain sense, immortal. They can clone themselves with absolute perfection. Thus death is not a natural and necessary mark of organic life . These primitive life forms do not die, except when they are directly attacked. We can even say that the reproductive cells of biologically developed beings, like ourselves, in some way constitute a horizontal line of immortal life. Sexuality may have led to individual death, but the species goes on indefinitely.

These observations show that life cannot be fully explained by the increasing complexity of matter and its mutation through energy, the reproduction and maintenance of equilibrium, and the loss of equilibrium through illness and death. Not even oxygen is essential. Some organisms have survived at the dark bottom of the oceans, for millions of years without light or oxygen. The bacteria of sulfate, nitrate, and nitrite, perhaps the oldest on earth, live without oxygen; indeed its presence might kill them.

So then, what is life? The mystery defies all our attempts to understand it. Life is spontaneity, movement, interaction, presence, energy, luminosity, and power. We respond to all of this by saying as the ancients did: we are in the presence of something not material, but spiritual. As we shall see later, life—especially human life—is the most amazing manifestation of the Holy Spirit in all creation.

Let us look first at life in the plant and animal world, and then at human life.

The Vitality of Plant and Animal Life

Scene one: Two kittens are playing with a ball. They run, spin around, tease each other. Then they forget the ball, and twist and turn together. They jump at each other with playful bites. They pull at the edge of a tablecloth; a vase crashes down and scares them away.

Their great exuberance and vitality show the real meaning of the word "animal": they are bearers of *anima*, the source of life and energy.

What we see in this familiar, everyday scene is life with all its vibrancy.

Scene two: In the Amazon rainforest, the pulsating energy that we saw in the kittens becomes a truly dionysian orgy of life. We feel it on our skin when we walk into the forest. We are awed and thrilled by the endless profusion of shades of green, seized and fascinated by the layers on layers of forest growth. Down below, small shrubs reach upward in their struggle for light. Climbing vines wrap their tentacles around tree trunks, weave in and out of the branches, rise, wave about, bend down and rise again, stretching out arms like long ropes, while their roots dig hungrily into the soil. Above us are huge, strong, grown trees, free of parasites. And above them, trees hundreds of years old thrust their heads proudly upward, held up by a mass of roots spreading out from three or four meters above the ground. The crowns of the high canopy hold court at the top, nodding at the clouds and raising proud faces toward heaven. Each of these great trees produces up to 300 liters of moisture every day, like airborne rivers that the wind will carry in different directions, bestowing rain or forestalling drought in faraway lands.

Amid all this strong, vibrant greenery the drama of animal life is exuberantly played out. There are myriads of butterflies, insects pollinating the flowers, every kind of animal. In the morning, at midday, and when they settle down in the evening, we hear the songs of birds, the roar of wild beasts, the chatter of parrots, the ineffable call of the *uirapuru*, the howl of monkeys, and the low growl of jaguars.

The people of the rainforest, small, frail, but brave, slip in and out among the rubber trees, watching out for the heavy Pará chestnuts that fall from the trees. They are filled with fear, reverence, and at the same time a sense of acceptance in the embrace of Mother Nature.

Life overflows everywhere around us, penetrating our being and forming with us an immense, vital, mystical body. This is the experience of life and the spirit that we find in nature.

The Radiance of Human Life

Life breaks through most intensely in the form of human life. We are amazed to find in it the most diverse dimensions of reality: physical-chemical, organic, psychic, emotional, rational, and spiritual. These dimensions are not layered on top of one another, but woven into a complex and multifaceted unity.

The whole history of life is present in different parts of the brain. The *reptilian brain*, over 300 million years old, is the seat of our involuntary movements: defense mechanisms, blood circulation, the beating of the heart, and the blinking of the eyes. Linked to that is the *limbic brain*, over 200 million years old; it emerged in the age of mammals, which carry their young until birth and build intimacy with them. The limbic brain brought something new into the universe: feelings, care, compassion, and love. We humans are rational mammals, charged with emotions and passions. Finally the *neocortical brain* evolved between 5 and 7 million years ago, giving rise to ideas and to the rational order of the world.

Human life is inhabited by energies, some of death, some of life and resurrection. On one side the power of self-giving love prevails. On the other is the negative power of aggressiveness and exclusion.

These energies coexist within us, because we are at once *sapient* and *demented* beings. Our ethical challenge as human beings is to strengthen the energy of wisdom and light over that of dementia and shadow, kindness over malice, hope over despair. For that reason human life is not linear but complex; sometimes we follow ennobling paths, while others lead us into shame.

The same dynamic is operative in social relations: different powers and interests coexist, sometimes in harmony, sometimes in conflict, and always in tension. In a way we reflect the whole evolutionary process, including chaos and cosmos, orders, disorders, and new orders.

The Human Being as Privileged Bearer of the Spirit

But the principal characteristic of human beings is our role as bearers of consciousness, of intelligence—in a word, of the spirit. The spirit infuses the whole universe from its very beginning, but in human beings it becomes self-aware and free.

The phenomenon that most particularly represents the spirit is human speech. Only humans, of all the higher beings, are endowed with language. We can even be defined as "the speaking being," as the Chilean biologist Humberto Maturana points out (*El árbol del conocimiento*, 1995). Speech recreates the whole universe of things, giving them names, codifying experience in phonetic and graphic symbols. In modern linguistics we can see the strict logic that regulates all language, even in the smallest child. We speak without needing to think about grammar and syntax.

The spirit is especially present in the language of love, in the poetry of nature, and in the rhetoric of persuasion. At such times, discourse is more than speech. It is transformed into *pathos, logos, eros,* and *ethos*, that is, into realities that move us, inspire us, convince us, and motivate us to take action.

In poetry the spirit irrupts as creation. Poets do not speak. They are spoken, by an inspiring energy that seizes their whole being. They sing life, they weep misfortune, they express secret experiences and reveal hidden intentions. They transform reality by means of metaphors and figures that evoke and bring life to amazing experiences.

An artist takes a piece of wood, cuts it, shapes it, and draws out of it an image that transports us to other worlds by conveying feelings of beauty and admiration. It is the transfiguration of matter. Especially in dance, bodies are transformed into spirit by the lightness of their steps and the delicacy and elegance they evoke.

But nothing shows the presence of the spirit in human life as well as love does. In love we seek to fuse our being with the "other." It is an act of unconditional self-giving that somehow resembles death, as it merges the identity of the "I" and the "thou." When love is expressed as compassion, the spirit enables us to come out of ourselves, put ourselves in the other's place, bend over the person fallen by the wayside. In forgiveness we transcend ourselves, so that the past does not have the last word and cannot close off the present and the future.

The highest expression of the spirit is the one that opens us to the Great Other, in love and trust. It establishes a dialogue with God, listens from the conscience to God's call, and delivers us trustingly into the palm of God's hand. This communion can be so intense, say the mystics of every tradition, that the soul of the beloved is fused with the Lover in an experience of nonduality; by grace we participate in God's very being. Here the human spirit is touching the hem of the Holy Spirit's garment.

Brilliant Flashes of Charisma

We see the presence of the spirit most vividly in charismatic believers. Charisma seizes them like a cosmic force. No one can find charisma, or build it. Charisma is like poetry: either it possesses us or it doesn't. Charismatics are inhabited by an energy that they cannot manipulate or control. It emerges and manifests itself through them. Some people are politically charismatic; they can carry away the masses by their fiery words, inventive metaphors, and startling gestures. In Brazil, former president Luiz Inácio Lula da Silva was an example of political charisma. Wherever he went, he could galvanize thousands of listeners with his powerful, creative words. There have been others. The charismatic influence of Gandhi, Che Guevara, and Nelson Mandela has lasted long beyond their lifetimes.

Charisma is expressed in the many activities of life, including the arts, music, theater, and film. The bearers of charisma naturally draw attention and produce fascination in the people around them.

Religious charismatics stand out from the others. By their very presence they transport us into the world of the Sacred; they make it possible to speak credibly about God and God's action in the world. There is an aura around religious charismatics that fascinates and gently draws people into their message. Dom Helder Câmara, Pope John XXIII, Pope John Paul II, and Martin Luther King Jr. were great charismatic figures. Religious charismatics renew old structures and give new life to ancient rituals. They nourish hope, recover the meaning of life in the midst of catastrophe, and become "the comfort of the people."

Spirit-Possessed Enthusiasm

Enthusiasm is one of the richest signs of possession by the spirit. There are two kinds of enthusiasm, as the ancient Greeks knew. One is a deeply human phenomenon, linked to exuberance for life and the love of life. An enthusiastic person takes initiative, overcomes obstacles, opens up new paths. Nothing great can happen without the power of enthusiasm.

The other is a power that possesses a person, a power that cannot be built up but only accepted. There is something of the divine in enthusiasm, as its etymology shows: it comes from the Greek *enthousiasmos*, which means to have a god (*theos*) within (*en-*). This energy *en-thuses* a person, that is, fills and moves the person with divinity.

Enthusiasm makes us sing, dance, laugh out loud, celebrate. Enthusiasm takes possession of poets, writers, actors, sculptors, musicians, painters, and makes them work by the power of creativity and inventiveness. That is the work of the spirit: transforming matter, borrowing sound to produce a melody, turning a chunk of marble into Michelangelo's Pietá or Moses. Out of the artist's enthusiasm come the works that inspire enthusiasm in their viewers.

The Irruption of the Prophetic Spirit and Poetic Inspiration

We see another great manifestation of the spirit in the prophets. These men and women are seized and driven by the Spirit. Their power is in the word that denounces the injustice perpetrated by the powerful on the weak and vulnerable. They attack unjust wages (Jeremiah 22:13), fraudulent business dealings (Amos 8:5, Hosea 12:8), the venality of judges (Micah 3:11, Isaiah 3:15, Amos 2:6–8 and 8:4–5), cruelty to debtors (Amos 2:8), economic exploitation (Isaiah 3:15, Amos 2:6–8 and 8:4–5), lives of ostentation and dissipation (Isaiah 3:16–23, Amos 6:5). They accuse kings of being bad shepherds (Ezekiel 34; Jeremiah 23:1–4). The prophet Nathan accused King David of having murdered Uriah in order to take his wife (2 Samuel 12). Jesus spoke as a prophet when he denounced the scribes for "devouring widows' houses" (Mark 12:40).

For this prophets have always been persecuted, imprisoned, tortured, and assassinated (Jeremiah 26:20–23, 1 Kings 18:4–13 and 19:10–14). But they also proclaim a new world, a new humanity and a new heart (Jeremiah 31:33–34), and a different spirit

(Ezekiel 36:26). They comfort and encourage the people (all of Second Isaiah, Ezekiel 37), in order to strengthen their faith and hope (Sirach 49:10).

Above all, the prophets are interpreters of crisis. They are extraordinary people who come into extraordinary situations (P. Bourdieu). They call attention to situations of social chaos and threats of war, and appeal for a change of life that can transform the situation. Prophets innovate; they seek to renew God's eternal covenant with God's people (Micah 6:1–8), and to transform a perverse reality with a right spirit and a new heart (Ezekiel 36:16–38). This is why prophets are always mixed up in politics: that is where injustice occurs and the needed transformations are possible.

Some modern prophets in the religious sphere have been Dom Helder Câmara of Recife, Brazil; Archbishop Oscar Arnulfo Romero, slain at the altar in El Salvador; Dom Pedro Casaldáliga in Amazonas; Dom Paulo Evaristo Cardinal Arns of São Paulo, the defender of human rights, especially for the poor; and Pope Francis, who has made life, tenderness, and compassion his central themes. In the social sphere, Leo Tolstoy preached active nonviolence and became a follower of Gandhi; Senator Teotônio Vilela denounced the Brazilian military regime and preached democracy; and the Brazilian Catholic thinker Alceu Amoroso Lima made public the practice of torture by the agents of repression.

There have been prophets in every age: in ancient Egypt, in Babylonia and Mesopotamia (Balaam in Numbers 22–23), and in every generation including our own. Wherever crises leave the people stunned and disoriented, prophetic voices are raised to point out new paths and build courage and hope. That is where we see clearly the transforming energy of the spirit.

The Power of the Spirit in the Face of Oppression

The spirit shows through in the courage of those who, like the prophets, denounce the powers that oppress society and marginalize the poor, and who also become their victims. Some engage in resistance and commit themselves to movements of liberation. Without passing ethical or practical judgment on all their tactics, we have to acknowledge that they have chosen the hardest path, filled with compassion for the victims of oppression. They are the ones "of whom the world was not worthy" (Hebrews 11:38), having suffered imprisonment, barbaric torture, and violent assassination. They did not bow down to the powerful. They did not compromise their ideals. They were faithful, and gave their lives for the sake of values that transcend life itself.

The Christian scriptures speak of *parrhesia*, that is, courage to stand up to the authorities, speak the truth boldly, and denounce injustice, in the name of the God of life and compassion for the poor. Like the prophets, many of these witnesses have suffered every kind of humiliation and sacrifice for their fearlessness. They spoke by the Spirit, with a power that could not be silenced.

Flesh and Spirit: Two Ways of Being

All these examples, and there are many more, help us recognize the presence of the spirit as life and energy. Some of its meanings can be mentioned only briefly. For example, we talk about the spirit of a people, the kind of life and culture we see in them. Or the spirit of the law: the deep meaning that goes beyond its letter. Or the spirit of an artistic form, such as the Gothic genre which points beyond itself to divine transcendence. Or we talk about a spirited person: one who is sharp, who draws unexpected connections and expresses a fine sense of humor. Or about the spiritual life, a life based on intangible values like communing with God, cultivating virtues, practicing love, solidarity, and compassion.

But there are forces opposed to the spirit, so we must always think about it dialectically. For every value there is an anti-value. The force opposed to spirit is not matter, but another spirit: an anti-spirit ruled by selfishness, hardness of heart, legalism, irreverence, and self-interested manipulation of the sacred. Scripture calls this "the flesh." People of the flesh live by an existential project that excludes the spirit of life, the spirit that shines with goodness and seeks whatever is right and just. The spirit and the flesh represent two different life projects.

People of the flesh are closed in on themselves, without concern for others; everything revolves around their inflated sense of self. The fate of the flesh is loneliness, rootlessness, and death. In contrast, people of the spirit live for others, open to love, and above all open to God and to everything sacred.

As we can see from this description, the concept of "spirit" is one of the highest that cultures have created to express humanity at its best, its capacity for transcendence and for life in all its forms. It shows us reality as becoming rather than being; it conceives of God as Energy and Dynamism, acting in the world, in history, and in every person. Traditional theology, in contrast, is based on a substantialist concept of God. It focuses on God's nature and essence as eternal, infinite, and immutable.

The concept of spirit invites us to see God as a process, as becoming, as the Energy that upholds the universe, humanity, and every person. This God is Action rather than immutable Substance; a God who makes a future by entering into history. History is not something apart from God; rather it exists to receive God, who does new things that have never happened before, such as incarnation. Through the incarnation God became what he had never been before, a God who steps out of mystery and reveals himself in the man Jesus of Nazareth. God the spirit is an open-ended reality, always in communication with everything. We also call God the primal Mystery, always knowable and always unknowable. Thus the Mystery expresses a dynamism that never does the same thing twice, but is always in the process of becoming.

All this evidence of dynamism and continual action leads us to think about the action, rather than the essence and nature, of God. God is always in relationship, a source of life, love, and unconditional self-giving. New manifestations of God are always being revealed in this endless ocean of energy.

Now we need to reflect theologically on these phenomena, in order to speak of the Spirit of God, of God as Spirit, and of the Holy Spirit as the Third Person of the Holy Trinity.

3

Spirit

Interpreting the Foundational Experiences

The phenomena discussed in the preceding chapter, which we call foundational experiences, call for interpretation. Each one has many interpretations, and none of them can fully explain or take the place of the experience. But the interpretations are part of the experience itself. Experience without interpretation is left incomplete, and in a way, silent. Interpretations reveal hidden dimensions that enrich the experience itself. They open a window to help us understand the spirit and the Holy Spirit. Let us look at some approaches to these foundational experiences.

Animism and Shamanism Are Still Relevant

Animism and shamanism are meaningful ways to understand our foundational experiences. According to a well-known expert on the subject, E. B. Tylor (*Primitive Culture*), they express "a well-ordered, well-articulated rational philosophy" (see also van der Leeuw, *L'homme primitive*, 25–162; van der Leeuw, *Phänomenologie*, 77–86; and Salado, *La religiosidad mágica*, 255–80).

Animism is a primitive mentality, not because it is old, but in the anthropological sense: it reflects one of the deepest, primal structures of the human psyche. Piaget showed that animism is the natural worldview of children (*The Child's Conception of the World*, 1926). In the winter a child sees the sun shining into the room and says: "How wonderful, the sun is coming in to warm our house!" Objects have life and intelligence. A child asks, "Why does the boat stay on top of the water, but a stone sinks?" Another child answers, in the best animistic style: "Because the boat is smarter than the stone" (Piaget, 210).

We modernists are also animists; we operate in the same primitive mentality when we express our experience of the world symbolically. Artists, poets, and painters know that very well. We experience our reality affectively, in a unifying, globalizing dimension, feeling ourselves part of the whole. Then we use metaphors like this one, from an Argentine tango: "I do not sing to the moon just because she shines; I sing to her because she knows how far I have walked." Here the moon becomes a companion, sharing our fate. We are animists, says the Dutch anthropologist van der Leeuw, "no matter how hard we try to forget it" (*Phänomenologie*, 82).

Everything speaks to us or sends us messages: mountains, forests, landscapes, colors, animals, our favorite household objects. Something radiates out of them and affects us, nourishes our imagination and enriches our experience. Objects have spirit because they belong to our *Lebenswelt*, our lived surroundings. The radiant energy of objects is well described by the word *mana* in Melanesian culture. Nagô tradition speaks of *axé* as the cosmic force that penetrates everything, which as we shall see later, is carried especially by the fathers and mothers of holiness. The ancients spoke of the *spiritus loci*, the spirit of a place, a landscape rich in memories. The fact that objects can live and talk is what makes poetry, painting, and all kinds of inspiration possible, even in formal philosophy.

Shamanism comes from the interpretation of reality as energy (Drouot, O *xamã*, 60–73). The shaman is not merely an enthusiastic person who does extraordinary things. He or she is infused with cosmic energies and, being so united with them, is led by them to do good things. Shamanism is perhaps the oldest cosmovision of humanity, through which human beings gave meaning to the forces of nature and felt deeply united with them.

The Biblical *Ruah*:
Spirit That Fills the Cosmos

The biblical writers described the energy of nature—wind, breath, storm, upheaval—as *ruah*. *Ruah* is spirit. Its manifestations are signs of life, vitality, movement, and the unpredictable, uncontrollable explosion of the forces of nature. What especially characterizes *ruah* is that human beings cannot predict or control it. Like all energies, it can have both good and bad effects. There is the Holy Spirit (found only twice in the First Testament: Isaiah 63:10–11 and Psalm 51:13), and there is also the spirit of falsehood and death (H. Duhm, *Die bösen Geister im Alten Testament*, 1904; P. Volz, *Das Dämonische in Jahwe*, 1924).

The story of Saul's prophetic frenzy shows the dominating power of the spirit. Saul is "turned into a different person" (1 Samuel 10:6). He pursues David to kill him. Three times he sends messengers. But the spirit comes upon them, and they are seized by a prophetic frenzy. Finally Saul himself goes out after David. But on the way the spirit also comes upon him: "He too stripped off his clothes, and he too fell into a frenzy before Samuel. He lay naked all that day and all that night" (1 Samuel 19:18–24).

Something similar happened with Moses and the seventy elders; they prophesied when the spirit rested upon them but had trouble coming out of their prophetic frenzy (Numbers 11:24–30). The spirit came upon Balaam, and he spoke an oracle describing God's plan for Israel (Numbers 24:3). 1 Samuel 16:23 speaks of "the evil spirit from God" that came upon Saul; other sinister, malevolent forces are also attributed to the spirit (Judges 9:23, 1 Samuel 18:10 and 19:9). The Lord even put a lying spirit in the mouths of Ahab's prophets, to entice him (1 Kings 22:21–23). As we see, the energy of the spirit can be either good or evil.

Nonetheless, the spirit gives Samson the incredible power to dismember lions, kill thirty enemies singlehandedly, and break his shackles (Judges 14–16). As Eduard Schweizer rightly observes, "Human beings possess a soul, but they are possessed by the spirit" (*El Espíritu Santo*, 23).

As we have seen, the spirit is manifested as a primitive force that breaks the conventional patterns of human behavior. It introduces the new, the unexpected, and the surprising. It is not a principle of institutional order and reinforcement, but of rupture and surprise.

Scholars have noted that the most ancient strata of the Bible are not very concerned with distinguishing among different spirits. Anything that can be truly described as a power, whether for life or for death, is called *ruah*.

Amazingly, this spirit is called *the spirit of Yahweh*. We have to remember that people came to this understanding within the animistic, mystical discourse that sees the world as filled with all kinds of energy. There is no moral judgment here. They simply observe that among all these energies there is a divine power, which in different circumstances may work for good or for harm. They are not thinking yet of a transcendent God, a foundational Energy that creates all the good energies that struggle against the evil energies in history. Later, Israel would slowly come to experience God the spirit as mercy and judgment, but always sovereign and transcendent, not a part of the comings and goings of this suffering world.

Thus the concept of *ruah* opens a window and a door to our understanding of the divine reality. In this sense spirit is used as an adjective, a characteristic used to describe something. This particular characteristic is found in nature, in history, in human beings, and also in God.

Two great French scholars, H. Caselles ("Saint-Esprit," 1990) and Jean Galot (*L'Esprit Saint*, 1991) have traced the roots of the word *ruah*. They found that its original meaning in ancient Semitic languages like Syriac, Punic, Akkadian, Samaritan, Ugaritic, and Hebrew was not wind, as had always been thought, but "the atmospheric space between heaven and earth, which may be calm or agitated" (Caselles, 131). This space later became the vital sphere from which all living beings, animal and human, derive life. This is the source of all the other meanings of *ruah*.

Its original meaning, therefore, is cosmological. Later it is expressed physically, as wind. Then it takes on anthropological meaning as the way human beings feel in their lived environment; in modern usage, a person might be in high or low spirits. In other words the spirit represents a divine vital energy, as we read in Psalm 104:29–30: "When you take away their breath, they die and return to their dust. When you send forth your spirit, they are created." Still later, God is described as spirit, because that is God's nature; and finally, the spirit becomes the Third Person of the Holy Trinity.

We shall come back later to the reality of the spirit in its theological sense, as the Holy Spirit.

Pneuma and *Spiritus*:
An Elemental Force of Nature

The Greeks had their own way of describing this foundational experience of cosmic energy. They called it *pneuma*, spirit as an elemental force in everything that exists and moves. It appears in nature as wind, in living beings as breath, and in human beings as *logos*, meaning an ordered, rational understanding of reality.

In this sense, *pneuma* is directly connected with life. It is also associated with the enthusiasm expressed in *eros*, which imparts life and love, inspires poets, and enlightens the thoughts of philosophers.

The Stoics in particular developed a worldview based on *pneuma*. It penetrates the whole universe, in the same way that the soul enlivens the whole body. It has the characteristics of divinity, because it cannot be controlled by human beings; rather, they are dependent on its manifestation. It is always present, but at the same time it is ineffable. Thus we speak of *pneuma* as *theion* or *theon*, a reality that carries divinity within it. Or more directly, as the Spirit of God (*pneuma tou Theou*). God appears as Spirit, as the source of life, intelligence, passion, and enthusiasm (Kleinknecht, *Kittel*, 7, 55). But *pneuma* is always seen in contrast with matter. It is immaterial.

Latin philosophy uses the word *spiritus* with the same meanings as the Greek *pneuma* and the biblical *ruah*: wind, breath, movement, and life. But like the Greeks, they understand *spiritus* as something immaterial.

The *Axé* of the Nagô and Yoruba Peoples: Universal Cosmic Energy

Nagô is the Brazilian name for the Sudanese African slaves from the Yoruba region, now a part of Nigeria (from Lagos north to the Niger River) and Dahomey. Many of them were taken by force to Bahía, where they became a hegemonic group whose language dominated those of the other African nations present in Brazil. Everyone who spoke the Yoruba language was called Nagô. Nagô was also a religion, syncretized in Bahía with Christian elements of the colonial and indigenous cultures. The core of this syncretism is not Christian but Nagô, because their identity so thoroughly prevailed over the other religious traditions.

It is a well-developed religion, with systematic theological concerns. Its central concept is *axé*, which parallels the Greek *pneuma*, the Latin *spiritus*, and the biblical *ruah*.

Axé is the energy that makes possible all the processes of nature and the emergence of human beings. People and objects can be the bearers of *axé*. It gives access to supernatural entities, or *orishas*, and keeps the community alive and active. More than substantive entities, *orishas* are the symbolic principles and models that rule over cosmic, social, and individual phenomena. These *orishas* (powerful energies) can be incorporated in people, who then go into a trance and become "horses," that is, the privileged bearers of *axé*.

Axé cannot be grasped. It is received, and it grows as its bearers become more open to it, as they enter into the world of their ancestors, celebrate the rituals, and are guided by the ethics and behavior of each *orisha*.

The supreme being is the greatest bearer of *axé*. His name is *Olorum* or *Alabá l'axé*, which means "the one who has the power of creation and realization." Below him are the different *orishas* and *exus*.

The figure of the *exu* in particular has been misinterpreted by Christians, especially by evangelicals, who see him as the embodiment of the diabolic. Because his *axé* is so intense, the *exu* is the principle of transmission, expansion, and diffusion of *axé*. The fathers and mothers of holiness, the priests and priestesses of the community, are imbued with a great power of *axé* and radiate it to others, producing beneficial effects.

Axé has a cosmic dimension. It penetrates all beings and processes, and it is transmitted to individual human beings in accordance with their openness and faithfulness. The blood spilled in the ritual sacrifice of animals is an expression of life, which must be defended, healed, enriched, and transfigured by *axé*. The density of *axé* in individuals leads them to cultivate a spiritual lifestyle and shape their lives in accordance with the virtues and behavior of their personal *orisha* (Elbein, *Os nagô e a morte*, 1976; Elbein, "A percepção ideológica," 1977, 543–554; Cacciatore, *Dicionário de cultos afro-brasileiros*, 1977).

Everything Is Energy:
Modern Cosmology

Finally, let us turn briefly to the interpretation from modern cosmology. In that interpretation there is no such thing as matter. Everything is energy. To speak of energy takes us to the heart of spirit, as we have broadly described it.

This is obvious to anyone with a minimal understanding of Einstein's theory of relativity, which equates matter with energy. Matter is highly condensed energy that can be released, as we saw to our sorrow in the atomic bomb and in the nuclear disasters of Ukraine, the United States, and Japan.

Science has followed an investigative path more or less like this: from matter it began to focus on atoms, then on subatomic particles, then on the Higgs Field, which gives mass to virtual particles like bosons and hadrons; these led to "wave packets" of energy, and then to supercords which vibrate in eleven dimensions or more, represented as music and color.

Thus an electron vibrates about five hundred billion times per second. All vibration produces sound and color. In other words, the universe is a symphony of sounds and colors. Finally, the supercords led scientists to the underlying energy, the quantum vacuum, a boundless ocean of energy with all possible virtualities and ways of being.

In this context the words of W. Heisenberg, one of the fathers of quantum mechanics, are worth remembering: "The universe is not made of things, but of networks of vibratory energy, emerging from something still more profound and subtle." Thus our focus is no longer on matter but on energy, organized in fields and networks. The spirit is becoming our central interest.

What is that "something more profound and subtle" that gives rise to everything else? Quantum physicists and astrophysicists call it "underlying energy" or a "quantum vacuum," which isn't quite right because it means just the opposite of a vacuum. Here the vacuum is the fullness of all possible energies, intensified in beings. Scientists today prefer the expression "pregnant void," or "the original source of all being" (Brian Swimme). It is not something that can be represented in conventional space-time categories, because it is prior to everything that exists, before space-time and the four fundamental energies: gravitational, electromagnetic, weak nuclear, and strong nuclear.

Astrophysicists imagine it as a vast ocean, without shores, unlimited, ineffable, indescribable, and mysterious, where all the possibilities and potentialities of being are kept as if in an infinite womb. From there, we don't know why or how, that tiny, pregnant point of incredibly hot energy exploded in the "big bang" that gave birth to our universe. It is entirely possible that that underlying energy could give rise to other tiny points, creating other singularities, other parallel universes, perhaps in another dimension.

Space-time came into being at the same time as the universe. Time is the fluctuating movement of energies and the expansion of matter. Space is not a static vacuum within which everything happens, but an open-ended process that allows the networks of energy and beings to become manifest.

The stability of matter presupposes a powerful underlying energy that maintains it in that state. Indeed, we perceive matter as solid because the energy vibrates too fast to be perceived with our corporal senses. But quantum physics helps us, because it reveals the particles, quanta, and networks of energy that show us this different vision of reality.

Energy is everything and in everything, just as *spiritus*, *mana*, and *axé* are in everything. Nothing can survive without energy. As conscious and spiritual beings, we are a complex, subtle, and extremely interactive manifestation of energy.

What is the underlying energy that manifests itself in so many ways? No scientific theory has been able to define it. Furthermore, we need energy to define energy. This leaves us in an inescapable redundancy, as Max Planck has pointed out.

As we shall see later, this energy is perhaps the best metaphor to describe the meaning of *Spiritus Creator*, God the Spirit as the Originator of everything. We may give it different names, but they all portray the same underlying Energy. The *Tao Te Ching* (§4) said something similar: "The Tao is like the eye of a whirlwind, always in motion, inexhaustible. It is a bottomless well, the origin of all things, and the power that unifies the world."

The uniqueness of humanity is our ability to enter consciously into contact with this primal Energy. We can call on it, accept it, and see it as life, radiance, enthusiasm, and love.

The Spirit in the Cosmos, in Humanity, and in God

We humans are unique bearers of this great energy, and therefore of spirit. In the perspective of the new cosmology, the spirit is as old as the cosmos. Spirit is the ability of all beings—even the most fundamental ones like Higgs bosons, hadrons, quarks, protons, and atoms—to relate to one another, to exchange information, and to create the networks of interconnection that make possible the complex unity of the whole. It is the spirit that creates ever higher and more elegant units and orders of existence.

The spirit exists first in the world, and only later in us. There is not a difference of *principle* between the spirit of a tree and our spirit. Both are bearers of spirit. The difference lies in the *way* we deploy it. In human beings, the spirit appears as self-awareness and freedom.

The human spirit is that moment of consciousness in which we become aware of ourselves as part of a larger whole, begin to grasp its wholeness and unity, and realize that there is a thread binding everything together and bringing a cosmos out of the chaos. By establishing a relationship with the Whole, the spirit within us turns human beings into an infinite project, wholly open to others, to the world, and to God.

In this way life, consciousness, and the spirit belong to the overall framework of things, to the universe, and more specifically to our galaxy, the Milky Way, the solar system, and the planet Earth. All this was made possible by a subtle calibration of all the elements, especially through the so-called laws of nature (the speed of light, the four fundamental energies, the electron charge, atomic radiation, the space-time curve, and others). If it hadn't happened that way, we wouldn't be here writing about it.

The astrophysicist Stephen Hawking explains it this way in his classic *A Brief History of Time*: "If the electron charge had been slightly different, it would have thrown off the balance of the gravitational and electromagnetic force of the stars, and either they would not have been able to convert hydrogen and helium or they would have exploded. One way or the other, life could not exist." Life is a unique moment in the cosmogenic process.

"The anthropic principle" (having to do with humanity) has been defined to help us understand this delicate balance of factors. It tries to answer the question that comes up naturally: Why are things the way they are? The only possible answer is that if they were different, we would not be here. But does that answer not lead us into anthropocentrism, the assumption that everything has to revolve around human beings, the center of everything, kings and queens of the universe?

That is a real risk. To avoid it, cosmologists distinguish between a strong and a weak anthropic principle. According to the strong anthropic principle, the initial conditions and cosmological constants were organized in such a way that at some given moment in evolution, life and intelligence would *necessarily* emerge. This interpretation would make human beings central. The weak anthropic principle affirms, more cautiously, that the initial conditions and cosmological constants were organized in such a way that life and intelligence *might* emerge. This formulation leaves the path of evolution open-ended, increasingly subject to Heisenberg's uncertainty principle and to Maturana-Varela's *autopoiesis*.

In any case, what we know is that after billions of years it did happen that way: life emerged 3.8 billion years ago, and intelligence between 7 and 9 million years ago. This is not a way of proving "intelligent design" or the intervening hand of Divine Providence. It only shows that the universe is not absurd; it is full of purpose.

There is an arrow of time that points forward. In the words of the astrophysicist and cosmologist Freeman Dyson, "It seems that the universe somehow knew that someday we would arrive," and was getting ready to receive us and set us on our way up through the evolutionary process.

The great mathematician and quantum physicist Amit Goswami supports the theory of a self-aware universe (*The Self-Aware Universe*, 1995). Something unique happens in human beings, he says, in which the universe looks at itself through us, contemplates its majestic greatness, and reaches a certain degree of fulfillment.

We should also remember that the cosmos is undergoing a process of genesis and self-construction. All beings have a propensity to emerge, grow, and flourish. That is also true of human beings. Humanity appeared on the stage after 99.96 percent of everything else was here. It is an expression of the cosmic impulse toward higher, more complex forms of existence.

Some people ask, but isn't it all by chance? We cannot exclude the role of fate, as the biologist Jacques Monod showed in his Nobel Prize–winning book *Chance and Necessity*. But chance does not explain everything. Biochemists have shown that it would take many billions of years for amino acids, and their two thousand constituent enzymes, to join together by chance in an organized chain and form a living cell. That is longer than the age of the universe and the earth. Perhaps our reliance on explanations from chance simply shows our inability to understand such higher, more complex orders as consciousness, intelligence, affect, and love.

In this sense, perhaps the most appropriate way to express the dynamic of the universe is the vision of Pierre Teilhard de Chardin: the increasing complexity of the universe gives rise to consciousness, and to our perception of an evolutionary Omega point toward which we are moving.

Should we not fall silent, filled with reverence and respect, before the mystery of existence and the meaning of the universe?

After these reflections, we are now ready to consider the theological dimension of the spirit as Spirit of Creation.

4

∽

Moving from the Spirit
to the Spirit of Holiness

In previous chapters we have looked at the various meanings of the word "spirit" (*ruah, pneuma, spiritus, mana, axé,* and vital energy). All these meanings are related to life, which emerges in unexpected ways. It is one of the highest concepts that all cultures have developed, and it has been applied both to humanity and to Divinity. They are spirit, or bearers of the Spirit.

The Spirit Acts in Creation

God also belongs to the domain of the spirit; it could not be otherwise. God above all. The Spirit is present on the first page of the Bible, which tells the story of the creation of heaven and earth. There it says that an impetuous *ruah* from God (wind, energy) swept over the face of *tohuwabohu* (chaos, the primordial waters) (Genesis 1:2). It brought everything out of nothing: inanimate beings, living beings, and human beings. Like everything else, humanity was formed from dust; God "breathed into his nostrils the *ruah* of life, and the man became a living being" (Genesis 2:7). The vital force of the spirit breaks through even more dramatically in Ezekiel 37: God's breath comes into the dry bones, covers them with flesh, and they come to life.

The noblest expressions of human beings are attributed to the presence of the spirit in them: poetry (in the Psalms and the

Song of Songs), wisdom and strength (Isaiah 11:2), the richness of ideas (Job 32:8), artistic skill (Exodus 28:3), the ardent desire to see God, with the consequent sense of guilt and repentance (Exodus 35:21, Jeremiah 51:1, Esdras 1:1, Psalm 34:19, Ezekiel 11:19 and 18:31).

God Has Spirit

This creative, energizing force belongs especially to God. The scriptures often speak of the spirit of God (*ruah Elohim*). Samson receives his great power from God's spirit (Judges 14:6, 19:15); God's spirit also gives prophets the courage to denounce the injustice suffered by the earth's poor, to confront the king and the powerful, and to proclaim God's judgment on them.

Jews of the intertestamental period expected the outpouring of the spirit on all creatures (Joel 2:28–32, Acts 2:17–21). The strong spirit of the Lord, with all its gifts, would rest on the Messiah (Isaiah 11:2).

In this context of later Judaism, a tendency arose to personify the spirit. It was still a quality of nature, human beings, and God, but its action in history was so intense that it began to take on an autonomous character. Thus, for example, the spirit was said to exhort, grieve, cry out, rejoice, console, rest on a person, purify, sanctify, and fill the universe. It was never described as a creature but as something divine that can become manifest in life and history, with transformative consequences.

God Is Spirit

This understanding began to change with the acceptance of a stronger expression: "spirit of holiness" or "holy spirit." This term is somewhat ambiguous, since it might be a way to refer to God directly without speaking God's name; Jews have always shown respect for God by avoiding the use of that name. "Holy" is the highest name for God in Jewish thinking, just as Greeks would call God transcendent, that is, different from every other being in creation.

We can say, however, that when the Jews described God as *ruah* (God has spirit, God sends God's spirit, the spirit of God), they were expressing the following experience: God is not tied down, but breaks in at will, upsets human plans, acts with irresistible power, reveals a wisdom that confounds all human understanding.

God comes in that way to the political leaders, prophets, sages, and the people, especially in times of national crisis (Judges 6:33, 11:29; 1 Samuel 11:6). God as spirit enables King David to rule with wisdom and prudence (1 Samuel 16:13)—and gives the same power to the suffering servant, who is utterly lacking in grandeur and majesty (Isaiah 42:1). "The spirit of the Lord God is upon me, because the Lord has anointed me . . . to bring good news to the oppressed, to bind up the brokenhearted, to proclaim liberty to the captives," the servant affirms in Isaiah 61:1. Jesus would later apply that text to himself in his first public appearance at the synagogue in Nazareth (Luke 4:17–21).

Finally, the term "spirit of God" describes not only God's innovative action in the world, but God's very being. The spirit is God, and God is Spirit. Because God is holy, the Spirit becomes the Holy Spirit.

The Holy Spirit penetrates everything, embraces everything, exists beyond all limitation. "Where can I go from your spirit? Or where can I flee from your presence? If I ascend to heaven, you are there; if I make my bed in Sheol, you are there" (Psalm 139:7–8). Evil itself is not beyond the reach of the Holy Spirit. Everything that has to do with change, rupture, life, and newness, has to do with the spirit. The spirit is so much a part of history, that history itself is transformed from profane to sacred history (Westermann, "Geist im Alten Testament," 229).

5

The Leap from Spirit
of Holiness to Holy Spirit

The revelation of the Spirit in history is a continuous process, which culminates in the Second Testament (New Testament). There the revelation reaches a level that has not been surpassed since then: God is revealed just as God is, personally, as a communion of divine Persons.

Revelation at this level is more than the communication of a particular understanding or a truth. It is the self-communication of the divine Persons. They step outside themselves, give themselves totally to others, and come to us just as they are, taking on our reality. The Father is personified in Joseph of Nazareth; the Son becomes incarnate in Jesus; and Mary is filled with the Holy Spirit.

Or we could say it differently, thinking about how God is internalized in creation: the Father slowly emerges in the evolutionary process until he finds a righteous, God-fearing father who can receive him. That is Joseph. The Son acts within the cosmic energies and then emerges fully in the man Jesus of Nazareth. The Spirit has always been moving things from one order to another, until it finds a woman "blessed among women" (Luke 1:42) who can receive it: Mary.

Let us retrace the main steps of the self-communication and externalization of the Holy Spirit, leading to its full recognition by the Christian community as God the Spirit. We will not analyze all the biblical passages, but they can be found in the theological writings of Congar, Schweizer, Moltmann, Kittel, Comblin, and others.

In the Second Testament we can see the different meanings that were identified earlier. Thus, for example, the anthropological meaning of the spirit (*pneuma*) describes the conscious, intelligent dimension of human beings: "At once Jesus perceived in his spirit that [the scribes] were discussing these questions among themselves" (Mark 2:8). Mary sings in her Magnificat: "My spirit rejoices in God my Savior" (Luke 1:47).

Pneuma also describes what the biblical writers called the heart, the essence of life. Thus, "Blessed are the *poor in spirit*, for theirs is the kingdom of heaven" (Matthew 5:3). That is: happy are they who have a humble heart, a self-giving attitude, and an openness to God and other people, unlike the Pharisees, who are depicted with a mean, contentious, and arrogant spirit.

Pneuma-spirit is also the vital principle of human life. When Jesus raised the daughter of Jairus who had just died, "her spirit returned, and she got up at once" (Luke 8:55); that is, she returned to life. At the death of Jesus, the gospel writers say he "gave up his spirit" (Matthew 27:50, Mark 15:37, John 19:30); that is, he stopped living and died.

In the intertestamental period there was a popular meaning of "spirit" as a ghost, a tormented soul. Thus at Jesus' resurrection, Luke reports that the disciples thought they were seeing a ghost (*pneuma*). Jesus reassured them, saying, "See that it is I myself. Touch me and see, for a ghost does not have flesh and bones as you see that I have" (Luke 24:39). Here a spirit is an imaginary, unreal, and disembodied phenomenon. "It is I myself" expresses the whole reality, life in flesh and in spirit. Similarly, an "evil spirit" is a synonym for the devil, the great adversary of life and the Kingdom (Mark 1:23, 3:11; Luke 8:27; Matthew 12:43, and many other parallels).

What Does Jesus Say about the Holy Spirit?

The historical Jesus says surprisingly little about the Holy Spirit in the synoptic gospels (Matthew, Mark, and Luke). He has the same attitude toward the Spirit that he has toward himself and

God the Father. He does not proclaim himself as the incarnate Son, the Messiah, and the Son of God. That is the message of the disciples, expressed in the gospels, but not the message of the historical Jesus. He does not talk *about* the Son, but acts *as* the Son of the Father; he is not proclaiming himself but the Kingdom of God. But he acts with the authority and displays the attitudes that reveal him as the Son of the Father, filled with the power of the Spirit and representing the coming Kingdom.

The same is true of his relationship with God. He does not proclaim a doctrine of God, but his behavior and his parables reveal an experience of God so intimate that he calls him *Abba*, or Father. This God is alive and active in history, on the side of the captives and those whose life is diminished. In the same way, Jesus is on the side of those whom society condemns, the sinners, the poor and invisible, such as women; he shows unconditional love and mercy to "the ungrateful and the wicked" (Luke 6:35). He calls God *Abba*, Father, because he knows himself to be God's Son. That is the self-perception of the historical Jesus.

Jesus seldom uses the word "Spirit," but when he does, it is to uphold life and liberation. If we understand the Spirit as the concrete and liberating presence of the God of life, Jesus did indeed live in the power of the Spirit, filled with its energy. He does not say much *about* the Spirit, but he lives, acts, talks, relates, and prays *in* the Spirit. He is fully the bearer of the Spirit, as foretold in the messianic prophecies.

He does mention the Spirit directly in his first appearance at the synagogue in Nazareth, where he introduces his liberating program with the text of Isaiah 61:1: "The Spirit of the Lord is upon me, because he has anointed me to bring good news to the poor. He has sent me to proclaim release to the captives and recovery of sight to the blind, to let the oppressed go free, to proclaim the year of the Lord's favor" (Luke 4:18–19).

Let us remember that this text comes immediately after Jesus' baptism by John the Baptist in the Jordan, where he had his foundational experience: "and the Holy Spirit descended on him" (Luke 3:22 and parallels). John the Baptist said clearly: "I baptize you with water for repentance. . . . He will baptize you with the Holy Spirit and fire" (Matthew 3:11). Luke adds that "the Holy Spirit descended upon him in bodily form like a dove. And a voice came from heaven, 'You are my Son, the Beloved'" (Luke 3:22). Later he says that "Jesus, full of the Holy Spirit, returned from the Jordan and was led by the Spirit in the wilderness, where for forty days he was tempted by the devil" (Luke 4:1–2).

The narrative suggests that the Spirit inspired Jesus' vocational experience, as he said at the synagogue at Nazareth. That was where his messianic consciousness came through clearly. The prophets said that the fullness of the Spirit would be upon the Messiah. He is the Anointed, the one designated as the Messiah, the Christ, not endowed with political, priestly, and prophetic power, but as a persecuted Prophet and suffering Servant. It is the Spirit that enables him to carry out his messianic task—the liberation of the oppressed, for which the people yearned so anxiously—but with none of the conventional means of power and domination.

We should mention the proclamation of "the year of the Lord's favor," the holy year which by biblical tradition should be celebrated once every seven years (Leviticus 25:8–54, Deuteronomy 15:1–11, Exodus 21:2–11). It was later postponed to once every fifty years. And finally, because it had never really been observed, the "year of grace" was projected into messianic times.

In that "year of grace" slaves were to be set free, debts were to be forgiven, and everyone forced by economic conditions to sell their land would be free to return to it. Also in that year, the land itself was to be allowed to rest. Jesus' promise to inaugurate the jubilee year, by the power of the Spirit, brought great joy to the Galilean people; they were all in debt, either through the taxes required by the empire and the temple, or through mutual exploitation among themselves. As a carpenter and peasant, Jesus must have experienced that harsh reality himself. What he was proclaiming amounted to a true, courageous, political, and social revolution.

There is another important reference to the Spirit in Jesus' reply to the Pharisees, who challenged his liberating practice: "If it is by the Spirit of God that I cast out demons, then the kingdom of God has come to you" (Matthew 12:28, Luke 11:20). Here the Spirit of God is the powerful presence and the divine energy that are inaugurating the Kingdom of God.

In a similar challenge to his practice of exorcism, Jesus is accused of casting out evil spirits "by the ruler of the demons" (Mark 3:22, Matthew 9:34, Luke 11:15). Here his messianic act is misinterpreted as a work of evil and wickedness. Jesus replies with one of his harshest and most mysterious sayings: "Truly I tell you, people will be forgiven for their sins and whatever blasphemies they utter, but whoever blasphemes against the Holy Spirit can never have forgiveness, but is guilty of an eternal sin" (Mark 3:28).

In this context, blasphemy is a direct insult to God or to an act of God. Jesus' hearers may have been offended by his humble origin, by his claim to be a bearer of the Kingdom, or by his disregard for the laws that forbade eating with sinners and touching lepers. That insult to the Son can be forgiven, because human beings do make mistakes and can be led into wrong judgments.

But the blasphemy of the Pharisees is that they know Jesus is an emissary of God, but refuse to acknowledge him as such. Their offense is not only their failure to recognize Jesus, but that they have attributed his works to the "ruler of demons," that is, the anti-Spirit. They also refuse to acknowledge the Spirit's ability to act on a man who has no power or material resources, but only his word and his call to conversion. Jesus appears in their midst as an insignificant man from the backwoods town of Nazareth. How can the Spirit work through a humble, powerless man like that? That is why his challengers demand an incontrovertible sign (Mark 8:11, Matthew 16:1).

Their attitude amounts to a dishonest, malicious, hard-hearted, and arrogant attempt to control the limits within which the Spirit is allowed to act. In fact, the Spirit blows where it chooses, and it chooses to act through the smallest and most vulnerable (Luke 10:21). As long as they persist in that obstinacy, they cannot be forgiven. God does not refuse to forgive them; God's mercy is offered to everyone, but they have emphatically refused to accept it (Congar 1974, 138–51). Only conversion can lead to their forgiveness. Without that, there can be no communion with God.

Another saying, which probably comes from the historical Jesus, occurs in the midst of a debate with the Pharisees. Jesus quotes the scriptural teaching that "David himself, *by the Holy Spirit*, declared, 'The Lord said to my Lord, sit at my right hand, until I put your enemies under your feet'" (Mark 12:36, Matthew 22:43–44). Rabbinic Judaism held that the scriptures were inspired by the Holy Spirit to encourage a holy life, to exhort, console, and strengthen faith in the God of the Covenant. Jesus belonged to that culture and affirmed that conviction: that the Spirit transforms human words into divine words, to produce the gifts of the Spirit. King David was speaking out of that divine power.

In another saying, certainly from the historical Jesus, we are told that "Jesus rejoiced in the Holy Spirit and said, 'I thank you, Father, Lord of heaven and earth, because you have hidden these things from the wise and intelligent and have revealed them to infants; yes, Father, for such was your gracious will'" (Luke 10:21). One of the gifts of the Holy Spirit is joy over God's action, which favors the smallest and least-noticed of God's people. Jesus was feeling that joy of the Spirit.

These words about mission and persecution are also certainly from the mouth of the historical Jesus: "Do not worry beforehand about what you are to say; but say whatever is given you at that time, for it is not you who speak, but the Holy Spirit" (Mark 13:11, Luke 21:14–15). The Spirit inspires those who are unjustly persecuted and taken to trial, with the words they need for their defense.

When Jesus sends out the Twelve (Matthew 10:5–20), or when he challenges the disciples to speak boldly (with *parrhesia*) before the tribunals, he says: "The Holy Spirit will teach you at that very hour what you ought to say" (Luke 12:12). The Spirit inspires the scriptures and also inspires people to live courageously what the scriptures teach.

Finally, these words are attributed to Jesus in his hour of temptation in the Garden of Gethsemane:"Keep awake and pray that you may not come into the time of trial; the spirit indeed is willing, but the flesh is weak" (Mark 14:38, Matthew 26:41). This reflects the Hebrew understanding of *spirit* and *flesh*. The spirit gives strength and shapes the whole response (body and soul) of those who are faithful to the Covenant; the flesh (the whole human being) is subject to weakness, temptation, and sin.

The Spirit Comes to Dwell in Mary of Nazareth

The Spirit was present in the original creation, which later entered into decline. We are sons and daughters of Eve and the old Adam. The same Spirit is present in the new creation that begins with Mary, the new Eve (Revelation 12:1), and with her son Jesus, the new Adam (1 Corinthians 15:45). For this reason the gospel writers attribute Jesus' origin to the Holy Spirit: the angel tells Joseph that "the child conceived in her is from the Holy Spirit" (Matthew 1:20). Luke says that the Holy Spirit will come upon Mary; it follows that the child to be born of her will also be holy (Matthew 1:35). As we shall see later, Mary becomes the bearer of the Spirit because she is filled with the Holy Spirit. Later we shall comment on this unique relationship of the Holy Spirit with Mary, and by extension, with women in general (L. Boff, *Ave María: O feminino y el Espiritu Santo*, 2003).

The Holy Spirit Forms the Community of Disciples

The community of Jesus' followers fell apart after his judicial execution. They all returned home in disillusionment, as we know from the young couple from Emmaus, probably a husband and wife (Luke 24:13–35). The women, however, never abandoned Jesus but stayed faithful, at the foot of the cross and in their attempt to care for his body at the tomb. It is the women who proclaimed his resurrection (Luke 24:9–10, Matthew 28:10), and their announcement of that blessed event was the beginning of the renewal of the community.

But the power to rebuild the community was the work of the Holy Spirit. In Acts 2, Luke tells about the restoration of the group of the Twelve, whose number carried an important symbolism: the regathering of the twelve tribes of Israel, representing all the peoples of the earth.

Luke's gospel has already introduced us to characters filled with the Spirit (Luke 1:41 and 67, 2:25–27). When Elizabeth heard Mary's greeting, she "was filled with the Holy Spirit" (Luke 1:41). At the birth and circumcision of John the Baptist, Zechariah "was filled with the Holy Spirit" and prophesied, singing the *Benedictus* (Luke 1:67–79). It was said of John the Baptist that "even before his birth he will be filled with the Holy Spirit" (Luke 1:15). Thus Luke tells us about the coming fullness of time, when the Spirit will be poured out on all flesh. The prophetic dry spell is over; the Spirit has returned and is active again. Luke describes Jesus as the Messiah, filled with the Holy Spirit, rejoicing in the Spirit because the Father is revealed to the little ones (Luke 10:21).

Luke summarizes his thesis in the prologue to the Acts of the Apostles: the Spirit that came to reside permanently in Mary (Luke 1:35) and then in Jesus will now be given to the disciples. "John baptized with water, but you will be baptized with the Holy Spirit not many days from now" (Acts 1:5). The Spirit that came upon Jesus will now come upon the messianic community. Later it will come upon everyone—"Even upon my slaves, both men and women," as Joel prophesied (Joel 2:28–32, Numbers 11:29, Acts 1:5; see Lina Boff, *Espírito e missão na obra de Lucas e Atos*, 102–27).

The Spirit is poured out, not only on communities but on individual prophets like Agabus (Acts 11:27–28), Philip (Acts 8:39–40) and his daughters (Acts 21:9), and Paul (Acts 13:9–11, 20, 23). It is the Spirit who inspires Philip (Acts 8:29) and Peter

(Acts 10:19–20) to evangelize even people of pagan origin. The same Spirit leads Barnabas and Paul into mission (Acts 13:2–4), and leads Paul to Macedonia in Europe (Acts 16:6–10). Luke interprets all these events as signs that the new times have begun, under the guidance of the Holy Spirit.

That interpretation sets the stage for Luke's story of Pentecost (Acts 2:1–13), although we don't know what historical sources he is drawing on. To Jews, Pentecost is the culmination of the great feast of Passover. For seven weeks they have been offering to God the first fruits of their harvest. Rabbinic Judaism had developed the idea of Pentecost as a time to celebrate the gift of the Sinai Covenant and its renewal for all the Jews dispersed through the vast Roman Empire.

Luke is drawing on different symbols from that feast. First, he uses the presence of many peoples, listed in the Jewish zodiac, to express the universality of the new message. Then he mentions the confusion of languages (Genesis 11:1–9), which left the peoples unable to understand one another. Now the Spirit comes down in the form of tongues of fire, and everyone understands the same message in their own tongues.

This nascent community, raised up by the Spirit, grows out of the story of Jesus. At the end of the Pentecost story, the people ask the disciples: "Brothers, what should we do?" Peter replies: "Repent, and be baptized every one of you in the name of Jesus Christ so that your sins may be forgiven; and you will receive the gift of the Holy Spirit" (Acts 2:38).

There are several important elements here. To enter into the community they must make a clean break, expressed as conversion. The Church is not an extension of the synagogue or of the human community as it now exists, a confused and divided Babel. Conversion leads to a new beginning of human history on a different pattern, in the Risen Jesus and in the Holy Spirit.

Why baptism for the remission of sins? Hasn't John already done that? Isn't the Holy Spirit enough? Here we see Luke as a perceptive theologian. Christians are called to follow the path laid out by Jesus. He accepted baptism and, in so doing, entered the messianic community (the original meaning of Jesus' baptism by John). More than a cleansing from sin, baptism meant that this new messianic people is holy, by the holiness of the Holy Spirit. That is why they receive the gift of the Holy Spirit. But the Spirit comes even before baptism; the Spirit is free, as we know from the case of the Roman officer Cornelius (Acts 10:44–48), or the Samaritans (8:17), or the disciples of John in the diaspora at Ephesus (19:6). But later they are baptized, because baptism is the sign of incorporation into the community.

Pentecost is the beginning, but not the end in itself. It continues and accompanies the community's mission at each step (Lina Boff, *Espírito e missão na obra de Lucas e Atos*). Luke is describing a bold vision: "But you will receive power when the Holy Spirit has come upon you; and you will be my witnesses in Jerusalem, in all Judaea and Samaria, and to the ends of the earth" (Acts 1:8). The Spirit spreads Pentecost in every direction. It does not distinguish between Jews and pagans. It is poured out on everyone who hears the message and is open to it, as happened in Caesarea when Cornelius and his whole family received the Spirit even before they were baptized. Perplexed by this, Peter tells the other Apostles in Jerusalem: "The Holy Spirit fell upon them just as it had upon us at the beginning" (Acts 11:15).

The Spirit is in the foundations of the new community that is being born. It introduces a new practice of life together, which we call primitive communism: "All who believed were together and had all things in common; they would sell their possessions and goods and distribute the proceeds to all, as any had need" (Acts 2:44–47). Luke adds with appreciation that "the whole group of those who believed were of one heart and soul. . . . There was not a needy person among them" (Acts 4:32–34).

The Spirit also establishes another way of living together: the missionary Church, which breaks through the narrow boundaries of Judaism and pushes out into the wide cultural world of Rome and Europe. The Apostles hold a council in Jerusalem to decide on the future course of the Church. Their decision is beautifully expressed: "For it has seemed good to the Holy Spirit and to us . . ." (Acts 15:28). It is the Holy Spirit who inspires functions (Acts 20:28) and assigns tasks (Acts 6:6, 13:2).

Who is the Holy Spirit for Luke the evangelist? Certainly he is not thinking in terms of the Council of Constantinople (381 CE), which defines it as the third person of the Holy Trinity. For Luke the Spirit is always the Spirit of Christ. It is connected to Christ, but it possesses a relative autonomy; it takes initiatives, irrupts as a powerful force to create new relationships, and inspires alternative economic practices (Lina Boff, *Espírito e missão na obra de Lucas e Atos*, 61–68). It is separate from the Son, sent by the Father and the Son, and always in communion with them. This shows clearly that for Luke, the Holy Spirit is God.

By affirming that the Father, the Son, and the Holy Spirit are God, we are not multiplying God; each person is unique, and unique entities cannot be added or multiplied. Rather it shows the centrality of the communion and love that swept into the world as a unique torrent of life, holiness, and liberation. Later theology formalized this idea as the doctrine of one God in three divine Persons, always interconnected, always in infinite communion and love (*perichoresis*).

The Holy Spirit Is God

It is in the Gospel of John that we find the most emphatic affirmations of the full revelation of the Spirit as Holy Spirit. First, John emphasizes the theological fact that the Spirit descended on Jesus and remained on him (John 1:32–33). This is his way of saying that Jesus is a permanent, not sporadic, bearer of the Spirit. John affirms that God gave the Spirit to Jesus fully: "He gives the Spirit without measure" (John 3:34). Because Jesus is full of the Spirit, he can also communicate it to others. He tells Nicodemus, "No one can enter the kingdom of God without being born of water and Spirit" (John 3:5). He says something similar to the Samaritan woman (John 4:10, 13–14), and later in the temple: "Let anyone who is thirsty come to me, and let the one who believes in me drink. As the scripture has said, 'Out of the believer's heart shall flow rivers of living water.'" John explains that "he said this about the Spirit, which believers in him were to receive" (John 7:37–39). Water is the great symbol of life. The Spirit is that life.

After his resurrection, Jesus breathes on the disciples and says: "Receive the Holy Spirit. If you forgive the sins of any, they are forgiven them; if you retain the sins of any, they are retained" (John 20:22–23). Here again the Spirit is linked to the new life that replaces life in the flesh. Jesus gives the Spirit, and promises that it will be fulfilled after his glorification. In this context he is speaking of the Spirit as the "Paraclete," or advocate. In the language of his time, "paraclete" means the defender of a judicial cause, or an intercessor before God for the achievement of a goal; it also means a helper in times of need or vulnerability.

John also calls it the Spirit of truth, which defends the accused and comforts the helpless (14:16, 16:7–11). In short, the Spirit upholds the testimony of Christians in a hostile world (15:26–27).

In his farewell discourse (John 14:15–31), Jesus promises (1) another Paraclete who already abides with the disciples (14:17); (2) that the Paraclete "will teach you everything, and remind you of all that I have said to you" (14:26); (3) that "he will testify on my behalf" (15:26–27); (4) that "he will prove the world wrong about sin and righteousness and judgment" (16:7–11); and (5) that "he will guide you into all the truth. . . . He will declare to you the things that are to come. . . . He will take what is mine and declare it to you" (16:13–15) (see Congar, *El Espíritu Santo*, 82ff.).

John adds, anticipating a trinitarian reflection that would come later, that the Spirit will be sent from the Father at the request of the Son; the Son will send the Spirit in his name (15:26, 14:16). The Spirit will not come until the Son goes away (16:7). Jesus also tells the disciples that the Spirit will always be with them (14:16) and will guide them into all truth (16:13). It is the Spirit who leads us to accept Jesus: "Every (human) spirit that confesses that Jesus Christ has come in the flesh is from God" (1 John 4:2). "By this we know that we abide in him and he in us, because he has given us of his Spirit" (1 John 4:13).

Finally, John says explicitly that "God is spirit." This declaration comes in a polemical context, in the story of Jesus' encounter with the Samaritan woman. Her challenge is: Should we worship God on Mt. Gerizim, the holy city of Samaria, or in Jerusalem, the holy city of Judaea? Jesus objects to such a specific location, and says: "God is spirit, and those who worship him must worship in spirit and truth" (John 4:20–24). In other words, God is not in any one place, because as Spirit he is everywhere. The important thing is not the geographic location, but the ability of the soul to worship in communion with the Spirit who fills all things and acts in history.

The Two Arms of the Father: The Son and the Holy Spirit

Now we turn to St. Paul's contribution to reflection on the Holy Spirit. He develops a clear distinction between the Risen One and the Holy Spirit. In his view, salvation comes through the dead and risen Jesus, and through the Holy Spirit. Human beings are called to be part of Christ and of the Spirit. The two are so united that we cannot speak of two economies, one of the Son and another of the Holy Spirit, as Joachim de Fiore and the Franciscan spiritualists would later try to do. They are the two arms of the Father; through them God reaches out to us and carries out what St. Irenaeus called God's plan of salvation.

Before we explore the pneumatology of St. Paul in more detail, let us emphasize the conviction shared by all the early Christians: we have come to the end times, and the new age of God is breaking in. Thus we are facing an imminent apocalypse. This is clearly stated in the earliest writing of the Second Testament, Paul's letter to the Thessalonians, written in 51/52 CE. In these end times, according to the ancient promises, the Spirit will be poured out on everyone as a divine power that will revolutionize everything, cleanse the world of all wickedness, and transfigure life and the cosmos.

Jesus' resurrection was the great sign that the Spirit was in action, inaugurating the new times foreseen by the prophets, especially Joel. The Spirit had made a dead man live, and had transfigured the living man. The apostles were preaching the fulfillment of the Reign of God in the person of Jesus, eliciting joy and commitment from many people. Pentecost must have been an extremely powerful, collective experience of the Holy Spirit in their midst. They saw the Holy Spirit as the source of their deeper understanding of Jesus' powerful act, and of their new vision of God as *Abba*-Father (1 Corinthians 12:3, Romans 8:15).

All Christians saw themselves as temples of the Spirit, who had raised Jesus from among the dead. They were sons and daughters in the Son: "For all who are led by the Spirit of God are children of God" (Romans 8:14, 8:29).

This framework of beliefs forms the basis of Paul's reflection on the Holy Spirit. Paul does not know the Church that was born at Pentecost, as Luke tells us in the Acts of the Apostles. He never refers to it. His experience of the Spirit comes from the existential shock of his encounter with the Risen One on the road to Damascus.

There he comes to understand that the crucified Jesus is the risen Christ, the Lord. "Anyone who does not have the Spirit of Christ does not belong to him" (Romans 8:9). What most impresses him is the new form in which Jesus now exists: not as flesh (*kata sarka*) but as spirit (*kata pneuma*). That is, the risen Jesus has taken on the characteristics of God, present everywhere in the cosmos and full of life. Later we shall see that Paul understands the spirit, with all its charisms and gifts, as the central axis of the Christian community, the Church.

Two Kingdoms and Two Projects: Flesh and Spirit

We can better understand Paul's reflection on the Spirit by looking briefly at the way he understands the human condition. We have done that in chapter 2, but it needs to be seen from

St. Paul's perspective. He uses two categories from the biblical tradition: *flesh* and *spirit*.

Paul says we live between two force fields, which are really two existential ways of living, each with its own direction or project.

The first force field is the *flesh*, the mundaneness of the world in its own terms, with no reference to anything else or to God. Life is socially organized in this domain, but it is marked by individualism and the pursuit of self-interest.

The other force field is the *spirit*, in which community life is lived with openness to others, centered on service and love. In his Letter to the Galatians, which was probably written in Ephesus around 56/57 CE, Paul emphasizes that the flesh and the spirit are opposed to each other:

> Live by the Spirit, I say, and do not gratify the desires of the flesh. For what the flesh desires is opposed to the Spirit, and what the Spirit desires is opposed to the flesh. . . . Now the works of the flesh are obvious: fornication, impurity, licentiousness, idolatry, sorcery, enmities, strife, jealousy, anger, quarrels, dissensions, factions, envy, drunkenness, carousing, and things like these. . . . Those who do such things will not inherit the kingdom of God. By contrast, the fruit of the spirit is love, joy, peace, patience, kindness, generosity, faithfulness, gentleness, and self-control. (Galatians 5:16–23)

He says it more clearly in the Letter to the Romans: "To set the mind on the flesh is death, but to set the mind on the spirit is life and peace. . . . Anyone who does not have the Spirit of Christ does not belong to him. . . . If the Spirit of him who raised Jesus from the dead dwells in you, he who raised Christ from the dead will give life to your mortal bodies also through his Spirit that dwells in you" (Romans 8:6, 9, 11).

If we live by the flesh, we are children of this world with all its decadence. If we live by the Spirit, we are children of God in God's glory.

According to the great biblical scholar Rudolf Schnacken-burg, "The term *according to the flesh* refers to our earthly, natural origin; the term *according to the Spirit* refers to our heavenly status, that is, the way of life of the risen Lord" (*Cristologia do Novo Testamento*, 40). To say that the Risen One is Spirit means that he belongs to the sphere of the divine and is the Son of God. Jesus lived in the flesh when he sojourned among us; that is, he shared our weak, mortal human condition. Paul tells Timothy that "he was revealed in flesh, vindicated in spirit" (1 Timothy 3:16); he uses the term Spirit to express the divinity of Jesus. Similarly, "No one can say 'Jesus is Lord' except by the Holy Spirit" (1 Corinthians 12:3).

"Lord" was the preferred name for God, as early as the Septua-gint. It has many nuances: theological (Jesus is God), cosmological (lord of creation), and political, because the Roman emperors gave themselves the title of Lord, and demanded to be worshiped as such. Paul was confronting the pagan theology and entering into direct conflict with the imperial ideology. We can see how dangerous it was to take that position.

Paul is expressing the divinity of Jesus when he calls him "the last Adam, [who] became a life-giving spirit" (1 Corinthians 15:45). He is also placing Jesus on a level with the Spirit, for as the Christian creed tells us, the Spirit gives life. Thus the Holy Spirit is God.

To live according to the Spirit is to live in the new reality inaugurated by the Risen One and confirmed by the mani-festation of the Spirit at Pentecost, a reality open to all the people and languages of the world. Paul establishes a direct equivalency between living in the fullness of Christ's deity (Colossians 2:9–10) and being filled with the Spirit (Ephesians 5:18); between speaking in Christ (2 Corinthians 2:17) and speaking in the Spirit (1 Corinthians 12:3); between "the love of God in Christ Jesus" (Romans 8:39) and "your love in the Spirit" (Colossians 1:8).

The Spirit, the Church, and Charisms

Being in Christ and in the Spirit is also at the heart of the Christian community, the Church. "For in the one Spirit we were all baptized into one body" (1 Corinthians 12:13). Therefore, our unity is built on the Holy Spirit, which gives it vitality and enables it to overcome any kind of bureaucratization. The community is described as a spiritual house (1 Peter 2:5). Each of us is a temple of God: "Do you not know that you are God's temple and that God's Spirit dwells in you?" (1 Corinthians 3:16, 6:19; 2 Corinthians 6:16). This means that human beings have something of divinity in them.

God is not far away, but in our life as a "sweet guest of the soul," as we sing in the old Pentecost hymn. Just as the risen Lord lives in us, so also the Spirit lives in and establishes communion with us (2 Corinthians 13:13).

This presence is made manifest in the different roles and activities of the Spirit in the Christian community. "We were all made to drink of one Spirit" (1 Corinthians 12:13). The Spirit allots its gifts to each one individually (1 Corinthians 12:11). "To each is given the manifestation of the Spirit for the common good" (1 Corinthians 12:7). No one in the community is useless. Everyone has some gift and performs some service.

For Paul, charism is not opposed to the institution. He sees the institution itself—a reality ordered and encouraged by its leaders to assure their cohesion—as a charism, for it offers a permanent service to the community. What is opposed to charism is not the organization but selfishness, arrogance, the dominance of a few over the community. That is why he warns, "Do not quench the Spirit" (1 Thessalonians 5:19).

Finally, we need to ask: Does St. Paul see the Spirit as a divine power, or as God acting in the world, in communities, and in each person? Although Paul is not yet consciously thinking in trinitarian terms, the reality he describes is indeed trinitarian. In some formulations we see the divine personality of the Holy

Spirit, who "searches everything, even the depths of God" (1 Corinthians 2:10); who is sent into our hearts (Galatians 4:6); who "bears witness with our spirit that we are children of God," so that we cry, "*Abba*, Father! (Romans 8:15–16).

When Paul says the Spirit lives in our hearts, he means it is something personal, living, divine, inside us (1 Corinthians 3:16, 6:19). It is God's free gift for us (Romans 5:15), the presence of God, giving himself to us and giving us life. Paul places the Spirit on the same level as the Father and the Son, which means that for him the Holy Spirit is God (1 Corinthians 12:4–6; 2 Corinthians 13:13).

From Signs to the Full Revelation of the Spirit

In this brief review of texts from the Second Testament—the synoptics, the Gospel of John, Acts of the Apostles, and the letters of St. Paul—we can see that the concept of spirit is used in different ways: as vital energy, breath, a divine transforming power in the cosmos, in history, in the people, in individuals, and finally in its full divinity, as God.

This created a problem for Christians from the Jewish tradition, whose monotheism was so strict that they would not even speak God's name; now they needed to rethink their understanding of God. Without abandoning monotheism—there cannot be more than one God—they began to develop a new way of naming God, not in static, substantialist concepts, but in terms of process, a way of life, always one but at the same time diverse (as in biodiversity). They learned to think of God as a communion of love, not in the loneliness of a single nature. This communion in love is so intimate and so radical, that the divine Three are unified (become one) in a single God-communion-love-gift-relationship.

The Spirit is something hidden in the heart of everything that happens in the cosmos, in history, in the life of every person, and in the poor; something that upholds, encourages and expands us, drawing us upward and forward, toward a final convergence in the Kingdom of the Trinity.

6

∽

From God the Holy Spirit to the Third Person of the Holy Trinity

Studying the sources of our faith, we can see growth and development in the early Church's reflection and discourse on the Holy Spirit, toward accepting its divinity. The Spirit is placed on a level with the Father and the Son in doxologies, at the end of prayers, in baptismal rites, and in the eucharistic epiclesis (invocation). The Church was not yet reflecting consciously and thematically on the divinity of the Holy Spirit, as we do today. It lived in a different time.

Its language is biblical, and thus focuses more on the work of the Holy Spirit than on defining its nature. The affirmation that the Holy Spirit is God comes out of the practice of faith and prayer. Let us look at some of the high points in this development.

The Baptismal Formula

The Gospel of Matthew, written around 90 CE, contains the formula for baptism: "Go therefore and make disciples of all nations, baptizing them in the name of the Father and of the Son and of the Holy Spirit" (Matthew 28:19). According to the best biblical scholars, this wording was added later and reflects early Church practice. The same formula also appears in chapter 7:1 of the *Didache* (around 50 CE); in St. Justin (*Apologia* I, 61); in St. Irenaeus (*Adversus Haereses* III, 17; *Epideixis* 3, 6); and in Tertullian

83

(*de Baptismo* 13). The trinitarian formula was so essential to the faith that St. Irenaeus, a great defender of orthodoxy against the heresies of his time, said that heterodox doctrines always denied one article or another of this trinitarian baptismal faith.

The Eucharistic Epiclesis

An epiclesis is a prayer of invocation to the Holy Spirit to transform the bread and wine into the body and blood of Christ. This invocation of the Holy Spirit to transubstantiate or transform the eucharistic species appears in ancient anaphoras, or rites of consecration: for instance in Hippolytus (our second canon), St. Basil, Serapion, the catecheses of St. Cyril (V, 7), and the liturgy of St. John Chrysostom. Only God can transform material elements like bread and wine into the body and blood of the Lord, that is, into something divine. This is the work of the Holy Spirit, whom the early Church believed in and affirmed as God.

Mission and Martyrdom

As Christianity expanded into different regions of the Roman empire in the post-apostolic period, suffering discrimination, persecution, and martyrdom, it often referred to the Holy Spirit. Believers prayed to the Spirit to give them courage to face the police and civil authorities and stand firm under persecution; and to give them wisdom and words of inspiration during their judicial trials, where they were accused of atheism and wickedness for denying the gods, especially those of each city, and for refusing to worship the emperor. Experience of the Spirit was a way of life for these Christians.

But as the persecution subsided, as Christianity came to penetrate the highest levels of society and even the army, and as it comfortably put down roots in the local cultures, it became increasingly forgetful of the Spirit. In general it is always that way: whenever the institutional Christian order and sacred power (*sacra potestas*) are dominant, then the community feels less need to invoke the Spirit to strengthen it. Routine takes the place of the creativity that comes from the Spirit.

Montanus of Phrygia was one of the Christians who noticed the change. In the year 156 CE he claimed to have been "sent by the Paraclete," and sought to arouse the enthusiasm of the Spirit in all the communities. He saw himself and his group as the fulfillment of the promised outpouring of the Holy Spirit and its spiritual gifts. He expected the age of the Paraclete Spirit to break through with him, which would mean the end of history and the fulfillment of the eschatological end times.

Montanism came to Rome from Phrygia, one of the most remote Roman provinces, and from Rome it traveled to Africa in the third century. Tertullian, the most creative and intelligent lay theologian in North African Christendom, became a fervent adherent. The montanists were very strict; they required brutal penances and long fasts, accompanied by extraordinary and convulsive phenomena (Congar, *El Espíritu Santo*, 94).

Tertullian introduced a distinction that would later become famous, between a Church of the spirit (*ecclesia Spiritus*), on the one hand, and a Church-number-of-bishops (*ecclesia numerus episcoporum,* on the other. The Church-Spirit was known for its enthusiasm and flights of ecstasy, the Church-number-of-bishops for its hierarchical organization and its power. Today we would say, a charism-Church and a power-Church.

St. Irenaeus went to Rome in 177 to talk to Pope Eleutherius, seeking advice on how to confront this framework of church models, which could lead to division. Their agreed-on solution was to strike a balance between a Church organized for different tasks and ministries, and a Church renewed by the gifts of the Spirit. Irenaeus said that "the Spirit is like a precious liqueur: served in a glass of good quality, it is renewed and brings renewal to its container (the Church)." He went on: "Wherever the *ecclesia* is, that is, the community, there the Spirit of God is also; and where the Spirit of God is, there is the Church and all grace" (*Adversus Haereses* III, 24, 1).

Monasticism: Men and Women of the Spirit

Monasticism was the most important source of spirituality in the post-Constantinian period (325 CE), in which the Church assumed political responsibilities and set out on a great and turbulent cultural venture, based on power. These were times of peace, because Christianity had been declared the official religion of the empire.

In veiled protest, fervent Christians such as St. Anthony, Pachomius, and others—led by the Gospel, the crucified Jesus, and the suffering Servant—left their everyday tasks and went into the desert. They wanted to live the spirit of the martyrs, since martyrdom no longer existed. They chose the desert because, in an old tradition, that was where the new earthly paradise would begin.

These men lived by the Spirit, cultivated the experience of God, and gave guidance to the faithful who came to visit them in their retreat. Even the Syrian stylites, who lived on the top of pillars, were known for their prophetic gifts and for their wise counsel to the faithful.

This movement gave rise to the religious life of men and women; in the West they were organized by St. Benedict of Nursia (480–543), now known as the father of monasticism. It took on new relevance with the rise of the great medieval movements emphasizing poverty, such as those founded by St. Francis of Assisi, St. Dominic, the seven Florentine saints, and the Servites in the eighteenth century.

Today we see an infinite array of religious congregations for men and women. These spiritual men and women are living the Gospel more as charism than as institution; among themselves they are creating conditions for the realization of the utopia promised in Jesus' blessings.

Theological Disputes: Is the Holy Spirit God?

The Holy Spirit had to "struggle" through many years of contentious debates before it was *officially* recognized as God and as the Third Person of the Holy Trinity. As long as people were praying and celebrating Eucharist, it wasn't a problem. The problems arose when reason became involved, attempting to reflect on and clarify the complex issues behind the prayers. That often happened far away from devotion and prayer, which are the best places to talk about the living, true God, and about the Spirit of life.

Debate over the divinity of the Holy Spirit began with the christological disputes that arose in the fourth century with the followers of Arius (250–336), the bishop of Alexandria, who could not accept that Jesus is divine in the same way that the Father is. The debate became radicalized between 342 and 360 when Macedonius, bishop of Constantinople, the primary see at the time, challenged the divinity of the Holy Spirit. They were called *pneumatomachians* (Spirit-fighters).

They were influenced by a kind of biblical fundamentalism, literally interpreting some words from the First Testament. There, as we have seen, the Spirit is viewed as an attribute—the power and vital energy—of God, but not directly as God. Thus they understood the Spirit as an intermediary or intercessor sent by God, with supreme dignity and holiness, to help us on the way to salvation; but for them the Spirit was not God, only God's most excellent creature.

The Cappadocians, who were among the greatest theologians of the orthodox Church (St. Basil, his brother Gregory of Nyssa, and his fellow student, St. Gregory of Nazanzius), energetically opposed this teaching by the most important bishop of the time. They wrote extensive treatises on the Holy Spirit, emphatically affirming that the Holy Spirit is truly God. St. Basil the Great wrote about the conflicts, and even death threats, provoked by the dispute (*Tratado sobre o Espírito Santo*, 182–83).

Another eminent theologian, Bishop Athanasius, entered the controversy with a letter to Serapion between 356 and 362, in which he based the divinity of the Holy Spirit on the baptismal formula. That formula expresses the formal entry of the Christian into the community, he said, and therefore it could not be mistaken. He concludes that the Holy Spirit is not of a different substance. It is God in the same way that the Father and Son are God, with the same substance. Basil the Great (330–79) carried Athanasius's argument further, in a treatise on the Holy Spirit that is still regarded as unsurpassed.

In September of 374, at a liturgical festival in Caesarea of Cappadocia, Basil composed a doxology that we still sing today: "Glory to the Father, to the Son, and to the Holy Spirit." He also wrote, in a more theological formulation, "Glory to the Father, through the Son, in the Holy Spirit."

Because St. Basil wanted to make it easier for the faithful to understand, and to save them the theological disputes about the word *homoousios* (of the same substance with the Father and the Son), he taught that by giving the Holy Spirit the same glory we give to the Father and the Son, we would be affirming the divine nature and equality of all three. He reasoned that if the Holy Spirit is not God, then we are not made fully divine, since that is God's will. But the truth is otherwise: the Holy Spirit dwells in us, works in us, enlightens us, comforts us, and inspires us in following Jesus Christ. Therefore, the Spirit must be of the same substance with the Father and the Son. They are all three, equally, God.

The Holy Spirit Is God:
The Council of Constantinople

In order to settle the theological debate, which was still enflaming the communities and their pastors and disturbing the public order, in 381 the emperors Gratian and Theodosius I convened a council in Constantinople, the capital of the empire. The emperors had given themselves the title of pope and demanded unity of doctrine for the sake of political cohesion in the empire.

The council brought together 150 bishops of the Eastern Church. After extensive debate they prepared a document (*Tomos*), which was later lost. We know about it indirectly, through a letter that the synod of bishops sent to Pope Damasus in Rome. He convened a western synod in 382, which reaffirmed the doctrine of Constantinople.

The bishops prepared a creed based on the one approved at Nicaea in 325. They began with a formula written by St. Epiphanius in his book *Anacoratus*, and added an affirmation of the divinity of the Holy Spirit: "We believe in the Holy Spirit, the Lord, the giver of life, who proceeds from the Father, who in unity with the Father and the Son is worshiped and glorified, who has spoken through the prophets."

Note that they did not use the expression ratified by the Council of Nicaea (325), which referred to the Son as *homoousios* (of the same substance) with the Father, but rather used language that presupposed that expression. In this declaration the Spirit is described as *Lord*, the name of God in the Septuagint. Another expression, "*Giver of life*," also emphasizes the action of the Holy Spirit. The Spirit is not only the gift but the giver of life, a role that can only be attributed to God.

The phrase "*Who proceeds from the Father*" was a way of opposing the heretical affirmation that the Holy Spirit was merely a creature of the Father. The Holy Spirit's relationship to the Son was not mentioned, since that was not yet involved in the debate; it would later become the center of the schism between the Orthodox and the Latin Churches. The creed says simply that the Spirit is "*worshiped and glorified*" with the Father and the Son. The Spirit has the same honor and glory, since it is on the same level with the other two divine Persons.

This all began with the doxology that had been prayerfully introduced by St. Basil the Great. The doxology led to theology, as an attempt to understand what was being celebrated; now we need to bring it back to worship and glorification, that is, to doxology. That is the only way to bring the mystery of the one and triune God out of the domain of abstract speculation, and transform it into what it should be: an invitation to love, glorify, and worship God in the best way possible.

Finally, the creed says the Holy Spirit "*has spoken through the prophets.*" This affirmation brings the Holy Spirit back into history, which as we have said, is its privileged field of action. It refers to the prophets, because it is in the prophets that we see the Spirit's action most clearly. Of course, its action goes beyond the prophets, into human hearts, history, and all creation. But the council did not discuss that wider picture; as a result, the creed focuses narrowly on the action of the Spirit in the religious domain (the prophets) rather than in history and the cosmos.

Now we have the Christian way of talking about God clearly delineated in trinitarian form: three divine Persons, Father, Son, and Holy Spirit, all one God. That leaves a great, challenging question for theological reflection: How should we understand this diversity-in-unity? This question forces us to set aside the Greek way of thinking about God and the world as separate substances, and think instead of the inclusive relationships and open-ended processes that characterize life in an evolving cosmos (L. Boff, *Trinity and Society* [1988] and *Christianity in a Nutshell* [2013]).

7

Paths for Reflection on the Third Person of the Holy Trinity

The creed of Constantinople (381) brought about a Church consensus on the divinity of the Holy Spirit, together with the Father and the Son. All the historic churches, East and West, old and new, accepted this doctrine, making it the center of Christian faith beyond all the theological and organizational differences in the Christian communities. Those who accept the trinitarian God are Christians; those who deny it are not.

But we still have different theologies and ways of theologizing, because each community is thinking within a different cultural environment, sensitive to different concerns. Thus there are several kinds of theology on the Holy Spirit. We not only think in concepts, but clothe those concepts in cultural images and symbols that guide our theological reflection and nourish our devotion. This reality is evident in our different liturgies.

Théodore de Régnon, a great historian of the mystery of the Holy Trinity, explained it well: "We are accustomed to thinking of the Greek and Latin churches as two sisters who love each other and visit each other, but have separate homes and different ways of living (*Études de théologie*, 3:412). Alexandre de Hales, the first medieval Franciscan teacher, wrote in his *Summa*: "The Greeks and Latins believe the same thing, but they each say it differently" (*idem credunt greci et latini, sed no eodem modo proferunt*).

For this reason it is customary to describe the differences schematically, despite the inherent risk of oversimplification. Such categories do facilitate our understanding, especially in the very demanding area of reflection on the Holy Trinity, which requires carefully chosen words and rigorous thinking.

Two Models of Understanding:
The Greek and the Latin

The Greek theologians begin with the concept of divine Persons, especially the Person of the Father, and move toward the nature of God. The Latin theologians begin with the divine nature, and move toward the concept of divine Persons. Thus the Greeks say, "Three Persons in God"; the Latins say, "One God in three Persons."

Both are expressing the same truth, but from different perspectives. The Latin theologians also say "one nature, personalized," whereas the Greeks say "three Persons in a single nature."

These expressions reflect different sociopolitical experiences. The Greek experience is marked by the centralization of power in the figure of an emperor, a satrap, or a tyrant. For them, God is fundamentally the Father. The Father has everything. He is the source and origin of all divinity (*fons et origo totius divinitatis*), which he transmits to the other two Persons. The Son and the Holy Spirit proceed from the Father, but in a way that does not envision the Father having two Sons. That would run the risk of subordinationism, making the Son and the Spirit subordinate to the Father, which the Greeks deny; they are trying to avoid that risk, as we shall see.

The Latins are coming from their experience with the Roman Senate, which divides and sometimes subdivides the power of the state.

They tend to think of God as a single, original nature, divided into the Persons of the Father, the Son, and the Holy Spirit. This leads to the risk of modalism: a single nature expressed in three different modes. It may also lead to the risk of tritheism: three "Gods."

The Greeks prefer to approach a mystery, especially the mystery of the Holy Trinity, by means of meditation, prayer, and liturgical celebration. They prefer an emotional line of reasoning, which respects the ineffable nature of the mystery rather than claiming to have grasped it rationally. They also use reason, primarily in an apologetic sense, as a way of defending the faith against heresies. But for the Greeks, divine truth itself is best attained in ways that go beyond reason, through devotion and worship.

The Latins have more confidence in rational analysis. They define theology as "faith seeking understanding" (*fides quaerens intellectum*, or *fides quaerens quaere*). Their theology, as exemplified by St. Thomas Aquinas and his followers, is more speculative than emotional. Thus they get wrapped up in endless debates that end up turning the mystery of the Trinity into an enigma, which interferes with worship and meditation.

Many of the theological differences between the Eastern and Western Churches are rooted in these different ways of feeling and thinking.

The Importance of Images for Doctrine

Abstract reasoning is always best understood and communicated by means of images and symbols, which help us grasp its content. Both Latins and Greeks use images to describe the divine Persons and the relationships among them.

The Latin theologians adopted the images of spirit and love as their primary reference points. The spirit helps us grasp the reality and shape it into an image. We distill this image into concepts (*conceptum*), which come from taking reality and spirit together as a way toward true understanding. Then we use words and voice to communicate what we have taken in and understood.

The medieval theologians applied this process to the mystery of the Holy Trinity. The Father is the absolute Spirit, with absolute self-knowledge. He projects an image of himself, through a word that expresses it totally. The Son is this image and this word. The Father not only recognizes himself in the Son; he loves the Son and wants to be one with him. The Son in turn recognizes the Father and wants to be one with him. The Holy Spirit is the union of Father and Son, the bond that ties the Father to the Son and the Son to the Father. A theologian of St. Augustine's time, Marius Victorinus, went so far as to call the Holy Spirit "the intercourse between the Father and the Son" (Congar, *El Espíritu Santo*, 115). Thus we have a circular image of the divine Persons. The Holy Spirit completes the circle of understanding and love between the Father and the Son. The Spirit is the creator of unity par excellence, the sweetness and joy of the union between Father and Son.

Another image used by some Latin theologians, developed by St. Augustine and continued by St. Bonaventure and others, is love. There is love, the lover, and the loved one. God is love (1 John 4:8). Love is always effusive, self-giving, and expansive. The Father is totally self-giving love. The Son receives the Father's love, and loves the Father completely. It is the Holy Spirit that unites the Father and the Son in love. The Spirit is also loved by the Father and the Son, and loves the Father and the Son. The Spirit is called *condilectus*, beloved by both the Father and the Son; together they constitute a single God-love-communion, mutual and eternal self-giving.

This image evokes the dynamic of love that goes outside itself, rests on the other, and because it is love, returns to itself.

The Greek theologians, preferring simplicity, use the image of human communication. The Father pronounces a Word that reveals him totally. This Word comes with the Breath that transmits it and makes it audible, understandable, and acceptable. There is no word without a simultaneous breath. In the Trinity, therefore, the Son is the Word that the Father speaks eternally to communicate himself. This Word is always accompanied and conveyed by the Breath (*spiritus* in Latin), or Holy Spirit. Thus the Son and the

Spirit come from the same Father but in different ways, one as Word and the other as Breath.

The Greek way of thinking is more linear. The Father is the source and origin of all divinity, which he transmits in its totality to the Son and the Holy Spirit (Breath) in different ways. Because this self-communication is total, we know that each of the Persons is the bearer of the same divine nature. The only distinction among them is that one is not the other. They are different so that they can relate to one another in love, a love so absolute that it unifies them into a single God.

The Controversy over the Origin of the Holy Spirit

The Latin and Greek churches accepted both these ways of understanding the Holy Trinity and the place of the Holy Spirit, without polemics of any sort. The controversy arose when they lost the sense of devotion and veneration, and began to develop a speculative theology that soon hardened into rigid, unbending doctrine. The cultural nuances within each formula were forgotten, and it became a struggle over the meaning of the words, as if everything depended on the words—and as if the words had only one meaning, the same meaning in all times and places.

The person of the Holy Spirit became the apple of discord. According to the Greeks, the Son and the Spirit come directly from the Father; according to the Latins, the Spirit comes from the Father through the Son, or with the Son, or by the Father and Son together. The Latins used the word *Filioque*, meaning "and through the Son." The Holy Spirit comes from the Father and from the Son. The Son, therefore, plays a part in the exhalation of the Holy Spirit.

The Greeks objected to this formula because it seemed that the Spirit would not have a single cause, source, and origin, the Person of the Father alone. The Son was also cause and origin; that was the reason for the *Filioque*. St. Thomas, an astute theologian, had tried to avoid this problem by saying that "the Holy Spirit proceeds mainly (*principaliter*) from the Father through the Son." But the Son still had a part in the origin of the Holy Spirit, and that was the Greek theologians' objection. Bear in mind that the focus was so heavily on the relationship between the Son and the Holy Spirit, that they forgot that the Spirit is also the Spirit of the Father. The Father is always the Father of the Son. And it is as Father of the Son that he breathes the Holy Spirit.

So far the debate had remained peacefully at the theological level, but it became an ecclesial conflict at Christmas, 808, when French monks from the Mount of Olives in Jerusalem inserted the *Filioque* (and from the Son) into the creed. The Greeks vehemently protested this violation of the agreement reached by all the Churches at the Council of Ephesus in 431, enshrined in canon 7: "Not one word of the common Creed may be changed, inserted, or taken away." The Latins were apparently not abiding by that agreement. An appeal went up to Pope Leo III. He forbade the insertion of the *Filioque* in the creed, although he supported the theological legitimacy of the term; thus the debate remained alive.

That relative peace was broken, however, in 1014 when Pope Benedict VIII crowned the emperor Henry II, and added the *Filioque* to the creed at the express request of the emperor. This reaffirmed the Western position with the support of the highest papal authority, which in turn was responding to the political power of the emperor.

Even the great protest that followed did not lead to a real split between the two sister Churches. The schism came about in 1054 in Constantinople, when the Latin cardinal Humbert accused the Greeks of having suppressed the *Filioque* in the creed. Not knowing the history, the cardinal forgot that the *Filioque* had been included in the creed through the arrogance of Pope Benedict VIII, to please the emperor. The Greek patriarch Photios, a better theologian than cardinal Humbert, denounced the collapse of the agreement reached at the Council of Ephesus in 431, and broke off relations with the Church of Rome.

The two patriarchs, Western and Eastern, then excommunicated each other. The two sister Churches became enemies and closed the doors and windows of their houses, until recent times when the excommunication was reciprocally annulled.

Later ecumenical councils, like Lateran IV (1215) and the Council of Lyon where St. Bonaventure was present (1274), reaffirmed the Western position on the *Filioque*: the Holy Spirit proceeds from the Father and the Son. From the Latin perspective, the Son's role in the exhalation of the Holy Spirit does not mean there were two principal causes. There is only one, the Father, but the Father transmits his own generative power to the Son. The Son only has what the Father has given him.

The aim of the Western position is to highlight the sameness of the divine nature. It emphasizes the equality of the nature of the three divine Persons. This avoids any risk of subordinationism. The Holy Spirit functions within the Trinity as the bond of unity between the Father and the Son.

The Greeks saw this as breaking up the unity of God the Father, which could lead to tritheism (three gods) or to binarism (Father and Son). For this reason Photios strengthened the Greek formula, saying that "the Holy Spirit proceeds *only* from the Father." In his view the divine Persons are not differentiated by their origin, which they all have in common—the Father—but only by the individual properties of each one. The result was a rigorous *monopatrism*, which complicated the dialogue with the Latin Church for centuries. It also gave added strength to centralizing, even tyrannical, political regimes, which became an extension of the monopolizing figure of the Father.

On the other hand, the Eastern theologians objected to the *Filioque* because it identified the Holy Spirit too closely with the Son, when as we said, the Spirit is also the Spirit of the Father and is always free by nature. This overly close association between the Holy Spirit and the Son had led to *christomonism* in Latin theology, that is, focusing only on Christ, to the neglect of the Holy Spirit.

Such an interpretation favored the centralization of power in the Church hierarchy, especially in the pope as representative of Christ and even of God. That in turn reinforced his jurisdictional primacy over all the churches of East and West, and finally his infallibility.

This interpretation was and is harmful to ecumenical dialogue, because it attributes exclusive authority to the pope. He is seen as a member of the college of bishops, but he is also above it and can act *ex sese*, that is, on his own behalf, without consulting anyone. This is called the *cephalization* of the Church (from the Greek *kephal-*): all power resides in the head. The sovereign, all-powerful head is represented by the figure of the pope.

To sum up the debate: the Latin theologians want to emphasize the unity of the divine nature, equally present in the Father, the Son, and the Holy Spirit. The Greeks want to protect the unity of the divine principle and origin, which resides in the Father (the source and origin of all divinity), without diminishing the specific qualities of each one of the divine Persons.

There are advantages and limitations in each interpretation. For the Latins the Spirit is always the Spirit of Christ; they forget that it is also the Spirit of the Father of the Son, who can act independently apart from Christ. The Greeks focus exclusively on the Father; this can lead to subordinationism, making the Son and the Spirit subordinate to the Father as their only source and origin.

In theological reflection today, especially in an ecumenical context, this addition of the *Filioque*—that the Holy Spirit proceeds from the Father and the Son—is considered superfluous. The basic reasoning is that when we say that the Spirit proceeds from the Father, we are always talking about the Father of the Son; there can't be a Father without a Son, or a Son without a Father. Father and Son are always together, and together they give shape to the Holy Spirit.

It follows that *Filioque* adds nothing to our understanding of the Spirit; we would do better to just leave it out (Moltmann, *The Spirit of Life*, 284). The circle of love and self-communication among the three divine Persons is already complete, with the Father, the Son, and the Holy Spirit as God-communion-love-self-giving.

Modern Efforts to
Rethink the Holy Trinity

Modern trinitarian theology understands the traditional terms (the Father as source, the Son as generativity, and the Holy Spirit as exhalation) as analogies and descriptions, rather than as objective realities. The indisputable reality of faith is this: God is not the loneliness of the One, but the communion of the Three.

Our words cannot describe such an august mystery. St. Augustine, the greatest teacher in this domain, acknowledges that "when we refer to the three divine Persons we must recognize the extreme poverty of our language; we say three Persons in order not to remain silent, not so we can claim to have identified the Trinity" (*De Trinitate* V, 9, 10).

But it is important to acknowledge that in speaking of the Father, Son, and Breath (Holy Spirit) we are assuming a logic of relationship. There can only be a Father because there is a Son. The Son leads us back to the Father, and they are both connected in communion and in love. The Spirit is the relationship between them, the love that unites, the Breath that goes from one to the other.

It is appropriate to begin with the Second Testament, which testifies to the Father, the Son, and the Spirit. Each one is separate from the other. They are irreducible. They are unique. To call each one God is not to multiply God; since each one is unique, they are not a number and cannot be multiplied.

But can they be three unique realities? God times three? That would be the heresy of tritheism. The important thing is to affirm that they are three unique realities. Unique realities cannot be added together, precisely because they are Unique. But they are always in relationship, mutually interpenetrated in communion and love. It is like a single wellspring that flows in three directions, each one a spring in itself.

Theologians use the term *perichoresis* to mean the interrelationship of the divine Persons among themselves, or their complete reciprocity (L. Boff, *Trinity and Society,* 134–36). In the beautiful words of St. Augustine: "Each one of the divine persons is in the others, and together they are only one God" (*De Trinitate* VI, 10, 12).

There is no hierarchy, no precedence, no causal order among them. They are simultaneously eternal and infinite. They emerge together, each one unique but always connected to the others, in such a profound and radical way that they become one. Together they are one God-love-relationship-communion.

They are different so that they can relate to and be with each other. Their relationship is one of revelation and recognition. Thus the Father reveals himself through the Son in the Spirit. The Son reveals the Father in the power of the Spirit. The Spirit reveals itself to the Father through the Son (*ex Patre Filioque*), just as the Son is recognized in the Father through the Spirit (*a Patre Spirituque*). The Spirit and the Son meet in the Father (*ex Filio et ex Spirito Patreque*). Thus their relationships are always tripartite and circular. Where one person is present, the other two are also (Evdokimov, *L'Esprit Saint dans la tradition orthodoxe*, 1969; L. Boff, *Trinity and Society*, 145–47).

Other theologians, such as O. Clément, T. G. Weinany, and R. Cantalamessa (*O Canto do Espírito*, 389–90), who do not think in terms of perichoresis and full reciprocity but seek to extend the tradition, prefer to use a different preposition in referring to the Spirit: not "from" but "in." The Son is born of the Father *in* the Spirit. It is *in* the Spirit that Christ cries *Abba*. The Son is always the Son *in* the Spirit.

But we should recognize that the concept of perichoresis is a better way to understand the relationship of the three divine Persons; it fits well with modern cosmology, which sees every-thing related to everything else in an intricate web of inclusion and reciprocity.

However we approach it, our goal is an inclusive, ecumenical interpretation that shows the circularity of trinitarian life, in which the Holy Spirit together with the Father and the Son make up the Kingdom of the Trinity.

8

Philosophers of the Spirit:
Men and Women

Culture, history, philosophy, and theology have always been accompanied by reflection on the spirit and on the Holy Spirit. Many people have written about it. Here we shall mention the names of only a few men and women who planted the seeds, and who continue to influence contemporary thinking on the subject.

Joachim of Fiore and
the Age of the Holy Spirit

Joachim of Fiore (1135–1202) was a Cistercian monk in Calabria. St. Thomas Aquinas called him an unpolished theologian, but he had great theological and spiritual insight. He gave voice to a perennial quest of the human spirit, a desire to understand the course of history and its transcendent meaning. One of his works is especially important, although it received little attention in his day: "A Harmony of the New and the Old Testament" (*Concordia Novi ac Veteris Testamenti*, begun in 1184). It was widely circulated after 1240, when a radical group of Franciscans called the "Spirituals" or "Little Brothers" (*Fraticelli*) adopted his ideas. They saw St. Francis as an embodiment of his thesis, the inbreaking age of the Holy Spirit.

Joachim de Fiore looked for symmetry and harmony in everything, in order to project a coherent vision of history. His basic thesis was this: "Because there are three divine Persons, there are also three states of the world." He and his later readers called these states "ages."

The first was the *age of the Father*, which began with Adam and continued through the patriarchs. This was the age of the laity. Then came the *age of the Son*, from King Josiah to Jesus Christ. This was the age of the clergy, the Church, hierarchies, and sacraments. The third was the *age of the Holy Spirit*, which began with the monk St. Benedict and would soon come to fulfillment. Then the eternal reign of the Gospel would be inaugurated; human beings would be completely spiritual and free. This was the age of the monks. The first was the age of the flesh; the second, of flesh and the spirit; the third, of the spirit alone.

This reading was adopted by the radical Franciscans who sought to live in strict poverty and saw themselves as sent by the Holy Spirit to implant the Eternal Gospel. They felt no obligation to the age of the Son, as expressed in the existing Church, its sacraments, and the Pope. In their view, all that was over; it had lost its legitimacy. Now was the time of the Spirit, which released them from all material, social, and ecclesial bonds, in order to establish the kingdom of complete freedom for the sons and daughters of God. The Eternal Gospel is the present and future of the world.

Of course, this view led to persecution and condemnation by the Church of the Popes, but that did not stop new, highly idealistic groups from forming. One of these was the "Brethren of the Free Spirit," whose masculine and feminine communities were called *beghards* and *beguines*. They lived completely apart, in extreme quietism, but enflamed by the idea of the presence and action of the Holy Spirit. Some of them boldly claimed that "the Spirit is incarnate in us every day" (*Spiritus Sanctus quotidie in nobis incarnature*).

Joachim de Fiore pioneered the idea of *renovatio mundi*, the renewal of the world, the break that would lead to the inbreaking of a new order. Since then the idea has never disappeared from the Church and from history. It draws hostility from supporters of the existing order, but it continues to inspire revolutionary groups, most of whom are associated with the oppressed and excluded sectors.

G. W. F. Hegel: The Spirit in History

The theories of the great German philosopher Hegel (1770–1831) draw explicitly on Joachim de Fiore. Hegel shared the same goal of formulating a total perspective, offering a coherent vision of history in all its aspects, from the history of nature and humanity to the history of the Absolute Spirit. He first attempted this systemic project as a young theologian in Tübingen with his book *The Spirit of Christianity and Its Fate*, which anticipated the basic theme of his famous book *Phenomenology of the Spirit* (1807): the reconciliation of human beings with nature, the objective spirit with the subjective spirit, and the universe with the absolute Spirit.

This fundamental theme came to him during a Holy Week in Tübingen, on a day he would later call his "theoretical Good Friday." The paschal mystery inspired the idea for which he is most famous: dialectical reasoning. In Holy Week we celebrate the life, death, and resurrection of Jesus. Hegel saw that as the fulfillment of a dialectic: *thesis* (the life of Christ), *antithesis* (his death on the cross), and *synthesis* (his resurrection). Thesis and antithesis are not simply opposites; they are surpassed (*Aufheben*) by becoming integrated into a higher synthesis. The synthesis in turn becomes a new thesis, which provokes a new antithesis, leading to integration in a new synthesis, and so on indefinitely. That is how the historical process works.

As we can see, there is a permanent movement here, an all-encompassing, uninterrupted dynamic. Hegel's philosophy begins with a theological affirmation, God as Absolute Spirit, but he places the Absolute Spirit in the dialectic that takes place in nature and in history. He rightly affirms that the meaning of life is not to be found in abstractions, but in the concrete reality of nature and history.

Nature and history are the scene of revelation, and also of the fulfillment of the Absolute Spirit and the human spirit. The Absolute Spirit, which exists in itself and for itself, is expressed in history, which encompasses the whole creation: nature, the human being, and the universe. The Spirit itself is enriched by going into exile from itself, because it reveals itself and creates a kind of mirror in which to contemplate itself. In this way it comes to absolute consciousness of itself. Finally it returns to itself, bringing with it all the reality that it has taken on. This totality is truth (*Das Ganze ist die Wahrheit*).

To put it in dialectical terms: the Absolute Spirit, in itself and in its reality for itself, is the thesis. Its manifestation in nature and history is the antithesis. And its return to itself, bringing with it all the achievements and embodiments of nature and history in which it has been totally submerged, is the synthesis which becomes a new thesis, creating an antithesis with which it forges a synthesis, and so on indefinitely.

This Hegelian insight introduces the idea of evolution as an underlying perspective. But it is not a mechanical evolution; it is animated by the Spirit, which moves it to increasingly higher, more meaningful orders, toward a supreme integration in the Absolute Spirit.

When Hegel speaks of the Absolute Spirit, he is not referring specifically to the Holy Spirit but to God the Trinity, which in itself is an expression of the divine dialectic. The Father is the thesis, the Son is the antithesis, and the Holy Spirit is the synthesis, the union of the divine persons in love and reciprocal communion.

Hegel's influence was and is still enormous. Everything is part of his synthesis, including the negative aspects of history (which belong to the antithesis). His language is hard to understand, but his goal is clear: to project a dynamic and all-encompassing view of reality which includes God, nature, history, law, aesthetics, and ethics, revealing to humanity its own grandeur and dignity. He once famously said, on becoming a professor of philosophy in Berlin: "We have been entrusted with the task of preserving, nourishing, and protecting the mystery of the Holy Light, so that what is most sublime about the human being will never be snuffed out and disappear."

Some theologians (Congar, *El Espíritu Santo*, 163; Welker, *El Espíritu de Dios,* 279) have criticized Hegel for borrowing excessively from Christian ideas of the Spirit, not making clear the role of the Third Person but subsuming it in the Absolute Spirit (God), and thus neglecting its close relationship with the liberating, redeeming work of the incarnate Son. Despite these limitations, Hegel's interpretation challenges pneumatology to think of the Spirit's relationship with the universe and its vulnerability, which has been practically absent from Latin theology.

Historically, Hegel's philosophy has given rise to two interpretations: the materialistic one of Marx and Engels, and the idealistic one that has nourished theology and the study of religions. The latter interpretation helps us understand history as the scene of the manifestation and fulfillment, not only of the Absolute Spirit, but also of the human spirit with its freedom and its ability to shape reality.

Paul Tillich:
The Spirit and Life without Ambiguity

Paul Tillich, the German-born US theologian and philosopher (1886–1965), is the Protestant thinker (he was a Lutheran) who has most strongly emphasized the Holy Spirit. He belonged to the Frankfurt School of philosophy and sociology. His life was committed to fundamental questions of culture and politics, along with specific issues in sociology, philosophy, and theology. As a member of the movement called "Religious Socialism" he drew suspicion from the emerging Nazi leaders, and was forced to emigrate to the United States in 1933. He taught at several universities, including Harvard from 1955 to 1962 and the University of Chicago from 1962 to his death in 1965. His way of doing theology appealed to many North Americans in different fields, with whom he organized open seminars and dialogues. Tillich was a prolific author. *The Courage to Be* and *The Shaking of the Foundations* are often quoted, but his best-known work is his three-volume *Systematic Theology* (*Teología Sistemática*), 1951–63.

Three of the most fundamental points in Tillich's theology are his method of correlation, the purpose of theology, and the ambiguity of all reality. Throughout his work he tried to translate theological concepts into the discourse of existentialism, creating a theology in secular language.

In Tillich's view there is always a correlation between the existential questions of human beings, and the answers given by the Christian message. The questions and answers are always related to each other. The Christian message is not "the sum of revealed truths dropped into the human situation like foreign bodies from a strange world. . . . The Bible is not a book of supernatural 'oracles,' completely apart from human reception" (*Teología Sistemática*, 61).

There has to be a correlation between the human search and the divine response. That means we have to begin with the existential human search, in order to discover the power of enlightenment and transformation that comes from the Christian response. Thus as we have seen, Tillich's work is marked by a conscious existentialism that takes human questions seriously; without them theology cannot give a fully adequate response. The method of correlation is fruitful, and is similar to the method used by the theology of liberation; it too begins by looking at reality, examining it critically, and using the word of revelation to shed light on the needed process of transformation.

Tillich's second point is related to the first, on human questions and divine answers: to define the purpose of theology. Throughout his vast bibliography, he emphasizes that human beings are always seized and pursued by one question: What is unconditionally important in our lives? What is our ultimate concern? He avoids using *ultimate, unconditional*, and *infinite* in an abstract sense. Rather he prefers to speak of our ultimate concern, our unconditional interest, our infinite quest.

This leads to his definition of the object of theology: "The object of theology is what concerns us at the deepest level; a proposition only becomes theological when it refers to its object in such a way that it can become a fundamental concern for us" (*Teología Sistemática*, 20). That is true of the question, "to be or

not to be" (22). The word "God" only has meaning if it means
what is most important to us, if it is the ultimate meaning in our
life, the life of the world, and the life of the universe.

This understanding keeps us always united with God and with
human beings in their concrete reality, full of anguish, in their
discovery of meaning that makes them happy and in the failures
that make their existence tragic. God is in this question, because
it has absolute importance for our lives. This is where theology
should begin thinking about God and the Christian message; this
is where it can generate meaning out of other meanings, and lead
us to the perception of an ultimate reality.

Tillich's third point is the ambiguity of everything real. This
represents the most philosophical dimension of his thinking. As a
philosopher in the great Western tradition, he says that everything
has an essence and an existence. Essence is the ideal, the pure
aspect of every reality. It exists in our understanding. In other
words, essence establishes the constellation of possibilities of a
reality. The essence of a tree—its treeness—represents an almost
infinite number of ways of being a tree. That is where existence
comes in. Existence gives reality to one of the many possibilities
offered by essence.

Thus there is an internal difference between essence and
existence, which means that any concrete reality will always be
ambiguous. It is not an essence, but only one of its possible expressions. Only one of the potentialities of the essence becomes real in
history; the essence always remains latent and open to other possible
expressions. This is the ambiguity of all reality: it reveals its essence
in different forms of existence. It is Being made real in different
beings, even though the essence and the Being are always hidden.

There is also ambiguity in the specific situation of a human
being before God. Human beings exist in a situation of decay, corrupted by the fall and by disobedience to God. On the other hand,
we are open to and in dialogue with God, because we never stop
raising the question of ultimate concern, of what is unconditionally important. We are divided beings, torn between our corrupted

existence and the endless search for God which inhabits our essence.

Applying this interpretation to life, Tillich affirms: "All the processes of life contain an essential and an existential element mixed together, goodness and alienation, so that neither one nor the other prevails exclusively; life always includes essential and existential elements; that is the root of our ambiguity" (*Teología Sistemática*, 466).

This situation raises the question: how to overcome our ambiguity? Can we ever hope for an unambiguous life? That is where, in Tillich's method of questions and answers, we hear the Christian message loud and clear: yes, we can hope for life without ambiguity. Tillich says: "The Christian message has produced three important symbols to express life without ambiguity: the Spirit of God, the Kingdom of God, and eternal life" (*Teología Sistemática*, 467).

The whole fourth section of his *Systematic Theology* is devoted to the Holy Spirit, the presence of Divine Life in the life of the creature. The Spirit is the *presence of God*. Presence is a key concept for understanding the action of the Spirit in history. Presence is more than just being there. It is the density of being, the being that always *is*, always becoming, seeking fulfillment, dispelling ambiguity. The Spirit penetrates the concrete reality; Tillich calls this "Spiritual Presence" (470–505).

This spiritual presence is manifested, first of all, in the human spirit which lives in the dimension of faith and love, and in this way is able to overcome ambiguity. It is also seen in human history, in the presence of Jesus Christ, the new Being.

In this context Tillich develops a suggestive christology of the Spirit (495–99). We see it in the spiritual community, mainly in the Church, which is penetrated by the new Being of Jesus. This is the space in which the unambiguous life becomes real.

He then discusses spiritual presence in three important areas: religion, culture, and morality. All three are functions of the human spirit; in each one he describes the inherent ambiguity of life, and the human desire to overcome it.

Beyond these human, personal, and collective dimensions, he also discusses spiritual presence in the organic and inorganic world.

This leads to a kind of cosmic pneumatology (596). However, he explains that "the universe is not yet transformed; it is still 'awaiting' transformation, but the Spirit is working the transformation in the domain of the spirit. Human beings are the 'first fruits' of the new Being; the universe will come later" (596).

The doctrine of the Spirit leads to the doctrine of the Kingdom of God as eternal fulfillment. The Presence of the Spirit prefigures this Kingdom, which is gradually being built by the ambiguous efforts of human beings, especially through the gifts of the Holy Spirit. This gives rise to an unambiguous reality in history, guaranteed by the Risen One and by his Spirit.

Tillich offers an excellent vision. We are always challenged by his way of entering into dialogue with the anthropological reality that he explains in the light of faith; many readers have found common sense and wisdom in his reflections.

José Comblin:
The Spirit as Liberating Life and Action

In Latin America the stage was set for a powerful reflection on the Holy Spirit by the irruption of the poor on the political scene; by *aggiornamento* in the Church, which began at Vatican II and was creatively pursued by the bishops at Medellín (1968) and Puebla (1979); and by the renewal of faith through the charismatic movements.

The most outstanding theologian in this area is José Comblin (1923–2011), a Belgian who lived in Chile and Brazil. He broke new ground in reflection on the Holy Spirit, at a time when the classical textbooks were focused mainly on its intratrinitarian relations, and on its presence in the Church. Comblin spent more than twenty-five years exploring the Holy Spirit, "trying to understand what it is doing on Earth and where it is working" (*A vida: em busca da libertad*, 8).

Seven of his books focus on the action of the Holy Spirit in the cosmos, in the world, in cultures, in religions, in persons, and in the Church: *O tempo da ação: Ensaio sobre o Espírito e a historia* (1982); *A força da Palavra* (1986); *O Espírito Santo e a libertação*

(1987; *The Holy Spirit and Liberation,* 1989); *Vocação para a liberdade* (1999); *O povo de Deus* (2002); *A vida em busca da liberdade* (2002). His swan song, *O Espírito Santo e a tradição de Jesus* (2012), was left incomplete and published posthumously. In that one he confessed: "Almost all my books have been commissioned by others. The only thing that came directly from me is this one, which I wanted to leave as a treatise on the Holy Spirit, that is, my small contribution to pneumatology" (*O Espírito Santo e a tradição de Jesus,* 23). Summing up all his work on this topic, it is fair to call him one of the great thinkers of the Spirit in the late twentieth and early twenty-first centuries.

This is not the place to discuss his practical pneumatology in detail. Here I will focus on the three volumes that directly address the topic of this book. Comblin discusses in depth the centuries-long tension between the Christianity that turned the Jesus Tradition into a religion (the Catholic Church, hierarchically structured around the sacred power) and the original Jesus Tradition (his evangelical legacy, the legacy of freedom, and the experience of God as *Abba* and unconditional love). The Jesus Tradition is a *movement,* rather than an *institution* which emerged in history with all its limitations and was later expressed in terms of power. Jesus did not come to establish a new religion; there were already enough of those. *He came to teach life.* His legacy is a practice, designed to engender new men and women, not to create pious members of a religious institution.

Comblin sharply criticizes "the class that has taken over all decision-making power, and marginalized the role of the Holy Spirit. In official theology the Holy Spirit governs the Church by means of the clergy. . . . The clergy has taken the place of the Holy Spirit. . . . But in the New Testament the Holy Spirit was given to all, and everyone receives inspiration, courage, and guidance from the Holy Spirit, even when they are not always faithful. That is the case with the clergy; history tells about enormous errors committed by popes, bishops, and priests, and Christians witness those errors every day" (161).

The challenge to Christians and to the whole Church is how to keep rescuing the Tradition of Jesus, which is not made up of doctrines and precepts. That Tradition has largely been lost or hidden by Christian concepts that distort or dilute it. Instead of a doctrine, Jesus left us a practice, a way of being before God (*Abba*), before others (everyone is a neighbor), and before the law (freedom), in the context of a great dream: the coming Kingdom, a Kingdom that will free creation from its decay, help lost human beings find their way, and reconcile the world with God. In other words, Jesus left us an absolute revolution that cannot simply be proclaimed, but that is being built with the help of those who try to follow the practice of Jesus.

Comblin analyzes the comings and goings of this Jesus Tradition: how it was diminished, and in some ways betrayed, when the clerical institution assumed imperial powers and became a power of domination rather than of service to life, especially the life of the poorest. Yet some people have always kept it alive, from the desert fathers and martyrs to the Christians today, inspired by the Jesus Tradition, who are committed to the cause of justice and dignity for all who have suffered injustice.

The titles of his two great studies summarize the themes we have just mentioned: *O tempo da ação: Ensaio sobre o Espírito e a historia* (A Time of Action: Essay on the Spirit and History, 1982), and *O Espírito Santo e a libertação* (1987; *The Holy Spirit and Liberation*, 1989).

The theology of liberation has developed a detailed christology, holding up Christ as the liberator of the poor and oppressed, and Christian practice as following the life, the cause, and the destiny of Jesus. It did not yet have a pneumatology, a more in-depth reflection on the Holy Spirit. That was Comblin's goal, which he accomplished in its fundamental aspects.

His greatness lies in his consistent pursuit of this theme, which is unique in the self-revelation of the Spirit: its creative, libertarian, revolutionary action in the Church, in society, and in the world. He places the theme in the context of "Liber-action Theology," that is, theology leading to action, action that makes freedom free at last from its captivity. This historic action is the work of the Spirit.

In fact there has been an undeniable, fundamental change since the 1960s: an irruption of the Spirit. It began in the evangelical churches, almost always in the poorer sectors; then, as we mentioned in chapter 1, it spread to our own Catholic Church.

Whether we like it or not, the charismatic movement represents a break from religious formalism, doctrinalism, and the clerical monopoly on the Word. Now the people are beginning to speak and act, to have experiences and ritualize them.

Comblin dwells at length on signs of the Spirit in the diverse actions carried out by the people, especially those who were historically humiliated and offended (*Holy Spirit and Liberation*, 51–75). For centuries they were enslaved, marginalized, and neglected, reduced to mere echoes of the voice of the powerful. Suddenly, surprisingly, they began to speak freely, in their own voices, with their own words. Dissident and revolutionary movements arose across Latin America, refusing to accept submission and silence any longer. There were and are thousands of Christians in those movements.

As they go on developing a strategy of resistance, especially in projects of liberation, their action is becoming more organized. They are courageously confronting military regimes and structures of national security (which really means the security of capital). They are no longer afraid. They are experiencing freedom and fearlessly suffering persecution, imprisonment, torture, exile, and assassination. This experience of freedom goes beyond the political dimension; it is also religious. They are emancipating themselves from ecclesiastical laws, the instrument of control by the clergy; they are establishing Biblical Circles and Ecclesial Base Communities in which they are the subjects of their own action, and other movements of action and reflection on human rights, faith and politics, and the role of women, indigenous peoples, peasants, and marginalized women (prostitutes).

One great sign of the presence of the Spirit is the creation of Ecclesial Base Communities. Says Comblin: "The community is a new discovery for all Latin Americans . . . a true miracle. . . . Its members are aware of a radical change in their way of life; this creates new personalities and enriches them in every way" (*Holy Spirit and Liberation,* 28). The primary experience of these communities is life, a new life, lived for the common good, for the transformations that can lead to a better, more just, and fraternal life. The goal is not to have more, although that is important in view of their widespread poverty, but to be more.

The people do not usually call this an irruption of the Holy Spirit. The oral tradition and catechesis they have received do not encourage that kind of deduction. What matters is not what they call it, but their experience of being seized by a new power, by an enthusiasm they have never felt before, which leads them to action. In theological language, it is the presence of the Holy Spirit. To bring it to consciousness and to interpret it to the communities are what theologians can contribute to the new evangelization. And they are learning the lesson. They invoke, accept, give thanks, and praise the Spirit present within them. That is why they often sing: "Let the divine Light come down on us," as we shall see in the final chapter.

Unfortunately we do not value the action of the poor, their work of life and survival, as highly as we should. They have been subjugated for centuries, as Comblin points out, turned into pew-sitters at church and workers for the powerful. They could never come forward with their own experiences, their situations, their words. What is new in our time is the irruption of the poor, so well described by Gustavo Gutiérrez and the liberation theologians. Comblin writes at length about this new reality, expressed in generative words such as *transformation, revolution,* and *liberation* (see all of chapter 7 of *O tempo da ação,* 268–98). The poor no longer accept the discrimination and oppression of the old order. And Christianity has become their ally, by siding with the poor against their poverty. All this is the work of the Spirit in history.

The role of theology is to grasp this newness and create a language capable of describing its spiritual nature—which cannot be grasped in static, substantialist categories but must be described as processes, movements, and new life, as we are trying to do in this reflection. That is Comblin's challenge to theology, not only in Latin America but in all churches.

St. Hildegard of Bingen:
Prophet, Theologian, and Physician

So far we have mentioned only men among the great thinkers of the Spirit. The male-dominated theological culture seldom paid attention to the women who were inspired by the Spirit. Perhaps they wrote less than the theologians, since it is only in the past two centuries that women have been able to come forward, attend theological schools, and write their own reflections. Today our experience of God and God's grace has been enriched by a vast theological literature, written by women from a woman's perspective.

St. Hildegard of Bingen (1098–1179), who was perhaps the first feminist inside the Church, deserves special note here. She came from a noble family in southern Germany, at a time of great political struggle among popes and emperors. It was also the time of the first crusades throughout Europe.

She was a genial, outstanding woman, not only for her time but for all times. She was the abbess of her Benedictine convent, Rupertsberg von Bingen am Rhein, a German prophet (*profetessa germanica*), mystic, theologian, a powerful preacher, composer, poet, naturalist, healer, dramatist, and writer.

Her biographers and other scholars still wonder how this woman accomplished so much in the constricted, male-dominated medieval world. Everything she did revealed her excellence and enormous creativity. Here are some examples from her works.

Theological and mystical writings: *Scivias Domini* (Know the Ways of the Lord), *Liber vitae meritorum* (Book of the Rewards of Life), *Liber divinorum operum* (Book of Divine Works).

Natural science: *Liber subtilitatum diversarum naturarum crea-turarum* (Book of the Subtlety of the Diverse Natures of the Crea-tures), in two parts: *Physica* and *Causae et curae* (Causes and Cures).

Music and poetry: *Symphonia armonie celestium revelationum* (Symphony of the Harmony of Heavenly Revelation, 77 pieces), *Ordo virtutum* (The Order of the Virtues), *Litterae ignotae* (Unknown letters), and *Lingua ignota* (Unknown language, an alphabet of her own invention).

Also miscellaneous works including a commentary on the Gospels, the Rule of St. Benedict, the life of St. Rupert, and almost 400 letters to popes, bishops, princes, monks, and family members.

Above all Hildegard was a woman with the gift of heavenly visions. She says in her autobiography: "In the 1,141st year of the incarnation of Jesus Christ, Son of God, when I was 42 years and seven months old, the heavens opened and a blinding light of great brilliance flooded into my brain. Then it burned my whole heart and my breast like a flame, not burning but warming . . . and suddenly I understood the meaning of the expositions of the books, that is, the Psalms, the Gospels, and the other Catholic books of the Old and New Testament."

Elsewhere she writes: "I simultaneously see, hear, know, and quickly learn what I know." She explains that her words are not like the words that come from one's mouth, but take the shape of a flame that goes deep in the spirit (Termolen, *Hildegard von Bingen Biographie*, 115).

How she acquired her knowledge of cosmology, medicinal plants, anatomy, and human history is a mystery. The kind of theology that comes as a gift of the Spirit is sometimes called "infused science." That term fits Hildegard perfectly.

She developed a curiously holistic vision, always mingling the human being with nature and the cosmos. In this context she speaks of the Holy Spirit as the energy that gives *viriditas* to all things. *Viriditas* comes from "green"; it is her word for the fresh greenness that marks everything penetrated by the Holy Spirit. Sometimes she speaks of "the immeasurable sweetness of the Holy Spirit, whose grace surrounds all creatures" (Termolen, 122; Flanagan, *Hildegard of Bingen*, 53). She has an evocative drawing of the Holy Spirit suspended above a harp. Beside it she wrote in Latin, "In You: Symphony of the Holy Spirit." Below, in German: "You are the harp of the Holy Spirit" (Termolen, 202).

She developed a humanizing image of God, ruling the universe "with might and gentleness" (*mit Macht und Milde*), walking hand in hand with all beings and watching them lovingly (Fierro, *Hildegard of Bingen and Her Vision of the Feminine*, 187).

In one text she refers directly to the Holy Spirit: "The sweetness of the Holy Spirit is immense and totally surrounds all creatures in its grace, so that no corruption in the integrity of its justice can destroy it, and shining, it shows the way and gives rise to rivers of holiness in the clarity of its power, without a stain of unreason. Therefore the Holy Spirit is a fire whose burning serenity, igniting the fiery virtues, will never be destroyed and will thus chase away all darkness" (*Ordo virtutum*, Fourth Vision).

She is especially known for her medicinal methods, which are still followed by some doctors in Austria and Germany. She reveals a surprising knowledge of the human body, and of the active ingredients of medicinal herbs as applied to different maladies.

Naturally her theological and prophetic activity drew the attention of the ecclesiastical authorities. Pope Eugene III read and approved her book *Scivias*. The bishop of Mainz said that "her doctrine comes from the Spirit, and her gift of prophecy is the same as that of the ancient prophets" (Termolen, 118).

Hildegard was not only educated and wise; she was able to organize her convent in the smallest details. For a time she directed two convents, her own in Rupertsberg and the ancient Disibodenberg, near Bingen, which she had entered as a young girl.

Her fame endures to this day, and her canonization was ratified by Benedict XVI in 2012.

Julian of Norwich:
God as Father and Mother

Another woman of note was Julian of Norwich (1342–1416), in England. We know little of her life, whether she was a nun or a lay widow. We do know she lived in seclusion in a walled cloister in the Church of St. Julian. At thirty years of age she nearly died of a serious illness. At some point she had visions of Jesus Christ, which lasted five hours. Immediately she wrote a summary of her visions, and twenty years later, having thought deeply about their meaning, she wrote a long and definitive version: *Revelations of Divine Love.* This was the first text written by a woman in English.

Her revelations are surprising because they are filled with unbreakable optimism, born of the love of God. She speaks of love as joy and compassion. She does not understand illness as a punishment from God, as many people did then; it is still a widely held belief in some groups. For her, illnesses and plagues are opportunities to know God.

She sees sin as a kind of pedagogy, in which God forces us to know ourselves and to seek God's mercy. Moreover, behind what we call hell there is a greater, always victorious reality: the love of God.

Because Jesus is merciful and compassionate, he is our beloved mother. God is also a merciful Father and a Mother of kindness. Says Julian: "The omniscient God is our sweet Mother; together with the love and kindness of the Holy Spirit they are one God and one Lord" (*Revelations*, 119).

For her, "the Holy Trinity has three properties: paternity, maternity, and lordship. Maternity belongs to the Second Person who is our Mother in nature and grace; she is our Mother in the form of our substance, in which we are rooted and grounded; she is our Mother in mercy and in our feelings. She is the Mother in many ways, and we are totally surrounded by her" (*Revelations*, 120).

The following quotation from her book shows the originality of her theology, the basis of a feminine theology: "God our Father is also our Mother. Our Father loves, our Mother fulfills, and the good Lord, the Holy Spirit, confirms. . . . It is good to pray eagerly to our Mother for mercy and compassion, and to pray to our Lord, the Holy Spirit, for his help and grace" (*Revelation*, 146).

Only a woman could use such loving, compassionate language, and call God a Mother of infinite kindness. Here again we see the importance of the feminine voice for a fuller understanding of God and the Spirit, who constantly surround us with their movement and their grace.

We could mention many other women: St. Teresa of Avila (1515–1582), Simone Weil (1909–1943), Madeleine Delbrêl (1904–1964), Mother Teresa (1910–1997), Sister Dorothy Stang (1931–2005), and so many others, bearers of the Spirit, moved by the Spirit.

We must also remember the anonymous bearers of the Spirit: those who comfort and wipe away tears, who offer words of consolation and discernment, who inspire and encourage others to do good works. They may not know that the energy acting in them is from the Spirit. The Spirit often works quietly from within, secretly penetrating the minds and hearts of people and groups, in order to fan the sacred flames of love, justice, brotherhood, and compassion, which are the gifts of the Holy Spirit.

In short, all these men and women and many other thinkers, bearers of the Spirit—such as Paul Evdokimov, Vladimir Lossky, and Olivier Clément in the Orthodox Church, and Jürgen Moltmann, Paul Tillich, and José Comblin in the Latin Church—have helped us capture the *dynamis*, the secret and mysterious Energy that penetrates the evolving universe and pushes it past setbacks and detours, toward a great irruption in the human spirit. It does so by anticipation and then fully, in Jesus, Mary, and the diverse religious, cultural, and moral expressions of humanity—throughout our life wounded by ambiguity, but already penetrated by the transforming Power of the Spirit, which guarantees a happy end for all creation. Then the Kingdom will be fulfilled, without ambiguity, in all its splendid glory.

9

The Spirit, Mary of Nazareth, and the Pneumatization of the Feminine

The self-revelation of God the Trinity is a self-communication: God's whole self is given over to the receiver, unconditionally. The receiver in turn is drawn in, made one with God. That is a top-down way of looking at it, from the Trinity to the human being and the universe. But we can also look at it from the bottom up, and from the inside out.

From the heart of the evolutionary process, always sustained and inhabited by the Trinity, the divine Persons well up in those bearers who have been prepared by the universe and by God's action to take one of the divine Persons into themselves.

The Spirit Comes and Dwells First in Mary

The culmination of the Holy Spirit's action came when it welled up in the life of a simple, devout village woman named Mary. The Spirit stepped out of its transcendence and took Mary into itself so radically that she was spiritualized (from the Latin term *Spiritus*) or pneumatized (from the Greek *Pneuma*). From then on she belonged to the Holy Spirit, and the Holy Spirit formed a single reality with her, without blurring the difference between Creator and creature. This unique event has a parallel in the self-communication of the Son to a man, Jesus of Nazareth, which led to the incarnation of the Son or the divinization of the man.

Luke's gospel describes this culminating event in the history of the universe and humanity: "The Holy Spirit will come upon you, and the power of the Most High will overshadow you; therefore the child to be born will be holy; he will be called Son of God" (Luke 1:35). Let us explore the meaning of this testimony.

In the first place, it shows us that the first divine Person to come into this world, to break into the evolutionary process, was not the Word or the Son but the Holy Spirit. The third Person in the order of the Trinity comes first in the order of creation. This is not my affirmation, but Luke's. It challenges us to overcome the *christomonism* that prevails in most churches and in scholarly theology, with its excessive emphasis on Christ, the incarnation of the Son, in the history of salvation.

The Spirit breaks in first, and is taken in by Mary. In the original Greek it pitches its tent (*episkiásei*) in her, comes to live with her permanently. This is not a prophetic irruption in which the Spirit seizes the prophet for a particular mission, and then leaves him. Here the Spirit comes to stay. Luke uses the image of a tent (*episkiásei* comes from *skené*, tent): the Spirit pitches its tent (*skené*) over (*epí*) Mary and dwells with her forever (Richard, "Conçu du Saint Esprit, né de la Vierge Marie"; Lyonnet, "Le récit de l'Annonciation et la maternité divine de la Sainte Vierge").

The same expression appears in the Gospel of John: "And the Word became flesh and lived [*eskénosen*] among us" (John 1:14). Here the Son breaks into the holy humanity of Jesus, which he received from Mary, and never leaves him; in Jesus of Nazareth the Son becomes one of us, like us in every way except in sin.

In the second place, it is only because of Mary's "yes," her "let it be done to me according to your word" (Luke 1:38), that we can speak of the coming of the Son to receive human flesh from Mary. The Son comes after, and is enabled by, Mary's full acceptance of the coming of the Spirit.

In the third place, we need to emphasize that "*therefore* (*dià óti*) the child to be born will be holy; he will be called Son of God" (Luke 1:35). The logical sequence is perfect: the Holy Spirit is taken into her person; she is raised to the level of God the Spirit; only God can beget the Son of God. Only Mary, taken into and identified with God the Holy Spirit, can bear a Holy One, a Son of God.

The Intellectual Blindness of Churches and Theologies

It is strange that none of the great theologians of our day, in formulating their detailed theologies of the Holy Spirit, even mention Luke's text about the coming of the Spirit to Mary. Jürgen Moltmann's excellent *The Spirit of Life* (1992) and Michael Welker's interesting *God the Spirit* (1994) leave this important passage (Luke 1:35) out entirely. Heribert Mühlen, a specialist in the Holy Spirit, cites the text three times in his 760-page *El Espíritu Santo en la Iglesia* (1974), but without mentioning Mary; he refers only to the Spirit's role in begetting the Son. Yves M. J. Congar, who wrote the most massive treatise on the Holy Spirit, *I Believe in the Holy Spirit* (1997, three volumes in French and one in English with 728 pages), mentions the text only in passing; he too never refers to the coming of the Spirit upon Mary, but only to the begetting of the Son of God.

It is true that our distinguished Belgian-Brazilian colleague José Comblin—in his intriguing *O tempo da ação* (1982), in the more systematic *O Espírito Santo e a libertação* (1987), and in his great posthumous work *O Espírito Santo e a tradição de Jesus* (2012)—does refer to the feminine and maternal dimension of the Spirit, but even he does not mention the Lucan passage on the spiritualization/pneumatization of Mary, or present her as the one who reveals the feminine, maternal face of God.

My point is simply to observe the blindness of a masculinizing, patriarchal theology to these texts, which speak of Mary and the feminine side of God. Some very outstanding theologians are affected by it. Their masculine blinders keep them from seeing these realities, rendered invisible and unimportant by our culture and our churches, which are only concerned with men and masculinity. God is masculine, Jesus is a man, and the Roman Catholic Church is led exclusively by men, usually men of advanced age. The anthropological categories of masculinity and femininity have not yet been discovered as important principles in the life of both men and women, and in our understanding of God.

Thus the great theological erudition of the European writers on the Holy Spirit is not enough. We also need a self-critical awareness of our social location and of the ways our masculinity conditions all our theological reflection.

More seriously, even most women theologians have internalized a masculine image of the Divine; thus they become hostages to the christology of the Son of God made man and fail to grasp the divine element in their reality as women. They have become dependent on the theology of men. They have not discovered, or known how to express, the relationship of the Holy Spirit to women's life and the role of Mary in the mystery of salvation, which shows us the face of God the Mother, of infinite tenderness and compassion. This omission on the part of women theologians only strengthens the excessive patriarchalism and *machismo* of the hierarchical Church, and holds back the struggle for the full liberation of women in society.

The Dwelling of the Spirit in Mary: Her Spiritualization/Pneumatization

The most immediate theological basis for identifying the affinity of the Spirit with the feminine, specifically with Mary, is on the first page of the Bible: "So God created humankind in his image, in the image of God he created them; male and female he created them" (Genesis 1:27). That is, something in God is responsive to both male and female; and something in both male and female refers back to God. The masculine and the feminine are both places for the revelation of God's nature; both are human paths that lead us to God, and divine paths that lead us to humankind, male and female.

We know that male and female should not be understood in genital, sexual terms (God is beyond sexuality), but as fundamental principles of human existence, qualities that are present in every man and every woman (*animus* and *anima*).

In Hebrew and Syriac, the word Spirit (*ruah*) is feminine. In both the First and the Second Testaments the Spirit is associated with some actions that are primarily (but not exclusively) considered feminine, relating to motherhood: conceiving, caring, helping, inspiring, protecting, accepting, forgiving, comforting. Even tenting or dwelling, *shekinah* in Hebrew and *skené* in Greek, was considered part of the feminine reality. In the First Testament, wisdom is identified with the Holy Spirit (Wisdom of Solomon 9:17), loved and sought after like a woman, a source of life, intimacy, and serene joy (Sirach 14:20–27).

The French theologian A. Lemonnyer has rightly said: "The Holy Spirit is the Divine Person who was 'given' to us in a special way, and is called the Gift of God par excellence. In the Trinity one of its names is love. These qualities belong to a mother more than anyone else, and in a way they define her. The Holy Spirit is the personification of love at its most selfless, most generous, most self-giving, like the love of a mother" (quoted by Congar, *El Espíritu Santo*, 597).

The Spirit Engenders the Holy Humanity of the Son

By the intimacy and density of its presence in Mary, the Holy Spirit revealed what it has always been in creation: the *Spiritus Creator*, the Creative and Generative Spirit that brought order out of chaos and penetrated all the creative movement of evolution. Just as the Spirit set the first creation in motion, now it engendered a definitive creation in the *novissimus Adam* (1 Corinthians 15:45), the Son of God in our human condition. The holy humanity of Jesus of Nazareth comes from Mary through the generative power of the Holy Spirit.

Let us not indulge our indiscreet curiosity about how this sacred event happened. We should reverently respect the biblical witness, which chooses not to go into such details.

The surprising and wonderful thing is that at this moment in history, a woman is at the center. A simple woman, uneducated like all the women of her time, but responsive to God's call and openly accepting the Spirit. Suddenly the Spirit draws her into itself, and she is pneumatized. She is the Spirit-bearer par excellence, for it has come to dwell in her permanently. The Spirit is acting through her. Therefore (*dià óti*) the humanity taken on by the Son, Jesus of Nazareth, is growing within her. Mary is the temple where the Spirit and the Son will dwell by the will of the Father of infinite mercy, who is also present in Mary's husband Joseph of Nazareth; in my view the Father was totally personified in him (L. Boff, *St. Joseph,* 2009). We can see the whole Divine Family, Father, Son, and Holy Spirit, in that humble, hard-working and devout family.

The Spiritualization/Pneumatization of Mary Radiates Out to Womanhood and All Creation

The spiritualization/pneumatization of Mary is not only about her. Mary belongs to the human community, men as well as women. We are all touched by this trinitarian event of infinite tenderness and mercy, revealed through the Person of the Holy Spirit. Something in us has become divine, brought into the Kingdom of the Trinity by Mary. Something of our warm, mortal humanity has become eternal.

Womanhood in all its expressions, ever since the emergence of sexuality two billion years ago, has been moving toward this culmination. Somewhere deep in the female nature, a welcoming cradle was being prepared for the arrival of the Spirit. At a given moment in history, when the time was right, it all opened up. That was when the eternal Spirit pitched its tent in Mary, a woman of the people.

The feminine side of both men and women was touched and spiritualized/pneumatized in this event. We have come to the fullness of time. We can see where evolution is going, although it is not yet fully realized; at that time women and the whole universe will achieve fulfillment and convergence.

Then the Kingdom of the Trinity, Father, Son, and Holy Spirit, will break through from outside and inside. From the beginning the Spirit has been working quietly within the process of evolution, to bring it to full fruition.

10

∽

The Universe

Temple and Field of
Action of the Holy Spirit

We turn now to a relatively new theme of pneumatological reflection: the relationship of the Holy Spirit to the universe as we know it today, through the new cosmology and earth sciences. Two books by Jürgen Moltmann, *The Spirit of Life* (1992) and *God in Creation* (1993), reflect an unusually wide range of elements from the new cosmology.

This aspect is almost absent, or touched on only tangentially, in most writings on the Holy Spirit. In Y. Congar's voluminous *El Espíritu Santo* (1983), only 10 out of more than 700 pages are devoted to the subject of creation. He cites important sources from the Fathers of the Church, but does not enter into dialogue with today's understanding of the world and its relevance to pneumatological reflection.

Few theologians bring this dialogue into their reflection, although we need it for a better understanding of God, the Trinity, and the Holy Spirit. I have attempted to do so in a book researched and co-written with Mark Hathaway, a Canadian expert in the new cosmology, titled *The Tao of Liberation: Exploring the Ecology of Transformation* (2013). The book received a gold medal in science and cosmology from Nautilus Book Awards.

The New Cosmology: An Overview

We begin with a simplified overview of the new cosmology, enough to identify the presence and action of the Holy Spirit in the process of evolution and in our life (summarized in L. Boff, "An Ecological View of the Cosmos," in *Cry of the Earth, Cry of the Poor*, 35–62).

One of the greatest revolutions in our understanding of reality occurred less than a century ago, when the scientific community noticed that change, not stability, is the natural state of the universe. In 1924 the US astronomer Edwin P. Hubble (1889–1953) proved that the universe is expanding. It all began with the "Big Bang," a great silent explosion (there was not yet any space to carry the noise) which still echoes today in microwave radiation from across the universe. Observing the light from the most distant galaxies, we know by their reddish hue (the Doppler effect) that they are moving away from ours. Calculating the speed of light, scientists deduced that the universe appeared about 13.7 billion years ago.

Thus we see an expanding universe, which becomes more complex as it expands; with complexity it becomes more inner-directed, which in turn moves it toward subjectivity and consciousness. It follows that a universe that has a beginning, that changes, and evolves will also have a history. That history can be told at different stages in its development. It is being told today by cosmology, astrophysics, quantum physics, and evolutionary biology.

We human beings also have a place in this process. Life, consciousness, intelligence, creativity, and love are among the manifestations of this cosmic history. Through us the universe can look at itself, think about itself, and wonder at its majestic beauty. Nothing in this universe is isolated, unconnected, or simply accidental. Everything is connected to everything else in an intricate network; thus we are all interdependent.

For the past 500 years, the dominant paradigm of a mechanistic, fragmented science has blinded us to these interconnections. We see things one by one, disconnected from the Whole, which erodes our sense of belonging to the real cosmic community—although that belonging was obvious and deeply felt by all the ancient peoples and cultures, especially our own indigenous cultures.

The Main Acts of the Cosmic Drama

Here is a summary of the main acts in this great cosmic drama.

Before there was a "before," that is, before space, before time (at point zero), before anything else, what was there? It cannot have been nothing, because nothing can come out of nothing. There was the Unknowable, the Unnamable, and the Mystery. Cosmologists use a term that means just the opposite of what the words say: what existed was the "quantum vacuum." It is anything but a vacuum; it represents the fullness of all the possibilities that may emerge and decay, that is, be realized in existing beings. Some use a more descriptive phrase, like "the original source of everything" or "the abyss" that gives rise to everything that has been or can be. Others, more specifically, call it the "deep energy" that preexists all other forms of energy and all other beings. It sustains and penetrates everything, causes everything to expand and evolve. We might describe it as a boundless ocean of seething energy, waiting to become.

Out of this "generative abyss" a tiny point emerged, millions of times smaller than the head of a pin, seething with energy at a temperature of many billions of degrees. At some moment beyond time, the point expanded to the size of an atom and then of an apple. Then suddenly, no one knows how or why, it exploded.

That unique event gave rise to an infinite number of elementary particles: hadrons, quarks, leptons, neutrinos, and others. They are all virtual, that is, particles of pure energy, without mass. Without mass there can be no matter. On July 4, 2012, the Large Hadron Collider of the European Organization for Nuclear Research (CERN) discovered the Higgs field in which the Higgs boson moves, which is sometimes called "the God particle." Matter emerges when elementary particles enter the Higgs field and acquire mass. The Higgs field is a kind of viscous fluid like the ether described by Aristotle and classical physics; it fills the universe, confers mass on the energy particles, converts them into matter, and thus continually creates the universe.

Theologically speaking, this "God's particle" is the means by which God created and goes on creating everything that exists. It would be a theological mistake to call it the "God particle," because God is not a particle or a part of the world, but rather the Creator and Sustainer of the world.

These particles, and the energy contained in the "big bang," exploded into a kind of cloud of energy and subatomic and atomic particles. Now space and time could come into being. Gradually the cloud began to cool, although its temperature was still a billion degrees. It expanded, and space and time expanded with it. The first nuclei of hydrogen and free protons came into being. Within the first half hour much of the original matter, from which we would all emerge, was formed with nuclei of hydrogen and helium, the simplest elements in the universe.

With that expansion the cloud cooled enough to become denser, and stable atoms began to form with their own nuclei and electrons. After a billion years, the shapeless cloud of energy and primordial matter condensed further and gave rise to large red stars. They burned for four billion years, consuming hydrogen and helium, and acting as huge ovens in which most of the physical-chemical elements we know were forged.

Then after all this time, they exploded into supernovas of breathtaking splendor. The elements were flung out in all directions, creating more space as they expanded. The supernovas became more concentrated, forming billions of galaxies, each one with billions of stars. The other physical-chemical elements came into being inside the stars: heavier elements like carbon, silicon, oxygen, nitrogen, and others. Among these stars was the first Sun, the forerunner of our Sun.

These stars also exploded, flinging out their elements and cosmic dust in all directions, over millions of years. Thus the present galaxies, stars, and our Sun were formed. The elements forming within them made possible the development of organic life, including human life. We all come from the same source. We are all linked and re-linked by a fundamental unity.

Two forces make the creativity of the universe possible, and hold it in dynamic equilibrium: contraction and expansion. The force of contraction is gravity, which limits the speed of expansion. Expansion is the force generated by the great explosion, which flings everything out in all directions. It did not have to happen just that way. If the force of gravity were a little greater, for example, the universe would have contracted into a black hole. If it were a little weaker, the great red stars could not have formed; life would be impossible.

The two forces limit and balance each other, making possible an ordered expansion that gives rise to increasingly complex, advanced structures. This suggests that the cosmos did not come about by chance. On the contrary, from the very beginning its evolution and endless creativity were sustained by these two forces.

Continuing Creation: Cosmogenesis

Creation did not only happen once, at the beginning. It happens through a continuing process of interaction between the two forces of attraction and expansion. For this reason we are not really talking about cosmology but cosmogenesis, the ongoing genesis of the universe.

This process of continuing creation goes through unique stages, each of which happens once and leads to all the others. Thus, for example, there was only one moment when the galaxies could have formed, not earlier or later. If that moment had not occurred, our cosmos would have remained an unstructured mix of energy and primordial matter. A universe like that would not meet the conditions for the emergence of life and consciousness. This shows that there is an underlying purpose in all processes, leading from one to another.

Thus from the beginning the cosmos was predisposed and oriented toward producing life and consciousness, at just the right time and at a certain level of complexity. If everything had not happened as it did, we would not be here reflecting on these things. Somehow the universe "knew" that life and consciousness would emerge, millions of years later.

The universe is always expanding, always creating, always self-organizing, moving toward ever higher and more complex orders, connecting everything with everything else.

The Cosmogenic Principle

The whole process of open evolution displays three characteristics, which express its internal dynamic. Together they make up the cosmogenic principle (*O Tao da Libertacão*, 387).

The first is its increasing *complexity*, or *differentiation*. This complexity first arose when two hadrons, two quarks, or protons came together; that relationship led to the creation of a new order. As the complexity increased, atoms, dense matter, cells, bodies, living organisms, and conscious, intelligent beings came into being.

The second characteristic is *interiority* or *subjectivity*. As beings become more complex, it seems that they turn inward and develop an inner existence. This leads to a certain subjectivity as each one establishes its way of relating to others, self-organizing, and entering on the historical scene of evolution. From this we know that all beings are historical; each in its own way participates in a cosmic, mineral, vegetable, or animal level of consciousness, and finally in the human level of reflective consciousness.

The third characteristic is the *interrelatedness* or *connectivity* of everything with everything else, which can be called a *Relational Matrix* or *communion* of the whole. The universe is not the sum of existing entities, but the relationship among all the existing networks that tie all the parts together, making us all interdependent. This gives rise to a universe that is one and diverse, dynamic and meaningful.

In the words of the renowned cosmologist Brian Swimme: "If it were not for *complexity* [differentiation], the universe would collapse into a homogeneous mass; if it were not for *interiority* [subjectivity], the universe would be an inert, dead place; if it were not for *interrelationship* [communion], the universe would become a collection of isolated singularities" (*Universe Story*, 73).

Thus everything is in motion, interrelated, and moving toward higher and more complex levels. Everything is in some way alive and full of messages. All beings can hear each other's history over the millions of years of evolution. The mountain converses with the wind, and with the energy of the sun and the cosmos. The woods and forests hear the voice of the rain, of the clouds, and of the communities—the quadrillions of micro-organisms, insects, birds, and animals—that live within them. It is human beings who can hear the message of all these beings, of the starry sky, and of their own hearts.

This means that evolution is not produced by accidental mutations, but by the primordial forces that create complexities, structured orders, and endless interconnections. The universe is upheld by the power of the cosmogenic principle, by cooperation among all things, and not by the survival of the strongest. Life spread across the planet Earth, not by the elimination of difference, but by relationships in which different beings exchanged matter and energy in a way that enabled the universe to become what it is.

The Living Earth, Gaia, Moved by the Energy of the Spirit

Let us skip over the stages of cosmic evolution and focus on our planet Earth. It emerged 4.54 billion years ago. Located at just the right distance from the sun, it possessed all the conditions for the emergence of life. Life developed 3.8 billion years ago, in some primitive ocean or ancestral swamp, in the form of a bacterium, the mother of all living things. Micro-organisms make up 95 percent of all living beings; there are more than ten billion of them in a single spoonful of earth. That was the beginning of an intense dialogue between living beings and the energies of the universe, the Sun and the Earth.

The atmosphere and the biosphere are creations of both the Earth and living beings, which made it a favorable habitat in which to reproduce. But scientific research shows that life is found not only on the earth's surface. Earth itself is alive; we call it Gaia, the name given by Greek mythology to the Earth as a living being. Many cultures express the same belief; until the dawn of the modern age they called her the Great Mother, or Pachamama.

Life entered a new stage of complexity between seven and nine million years ago with the emergence of Australopithecus, an anthropoid ancestor with some characteristics foreshadowing human nature. Humanity itself appeared some 150,000 years ago with the emergence of our own species, *Homo sapiens sapiens*.

In the 1950s, with the discovery of DNA in living cells, we began to learn something surprising: all living organisms—from the most primitive bacteria, to forests and dinosaurs, to human beings—are formed out of the physical-chemical elements that developed in the heart of the great red stars and supernovas. We all share the same basic genetic alphabet: twenty amino acids and four nucleobases. That means we are all relatives, one another's brothers and sisters; we are all part of the great community of life, part of the earthly and cosmic community.

Consciousness and spirit represent the culmination of the cosmogenic process. Since intelligent, conscious beings are part of the universe, it is through us that the universe perceives and thinks about itself. When we look at the starry sky, or at the exuberant immensity of the Amazon basin traversed by immense rivers, through us the universe is seeing itself and marveling at its indescribable beauty. We have spirit and consciousness because they were already here in the universe. Through us the universe is aware of itself, and this awareness grows along with our ability to broaden the horizons of our minds and our hearts.

The Purpose of the Cosmogenic Process

We have seen that there is deep and coherent meaning in the evolutionary process, as if there were a kind of "attractor" that pulls all beings in a specific direction. We evolved from the original energies into subatomic particles; then into atoms that coalesced into separate entities and, later, organisms; from organisms into more complex vertebrates with a diffuse consciousness, and then to the reflective consciousness of human beings. We have to see an upward-pointing arrow here. And today we are moving from the local to the national, from the national to the global, from the global to the universal, open to totality, recognizing ourselves as an important chapter in the history of the universe.

Something about human beings refuses to think of things as simply scattered about, thrown together any which way. They see an organizing principle that brings things together to form a cosmos instead of chaos. They sense that a powerful and loving Energy is in action, upholding, preserving, and moving things forward together. They dare to give a name to this mysterious and fascinating reality. They give it names inspired by veneration and respect. What is more they can enter into dialogue with it, celebrate it with rituals, dances, and feasts. They feel it as an inner *enthusiasm* (from the Greek word for a "god" within). It inspires feelings of reverence, devotion, and worship.

Today's neuroscientists have identified what they call a "God point" in the brain (Zohar, *La inteligência espiritual*, 2000). They have observed a spike of activity in the frontal lobes of the brain whenever human beings, male or female, are confronted with what they consider absolutely important (what Paul Tillich called "ultimate concern," as we saw earlier), or a feeling of connection with the Whole.

This suggests an evolutionary advantage: human beings are able to perceive the presence of the Mysterious and Ineffable in reality. We respond with attitudes of respect and reverent silence. Just as we have external sense organs that enable us to see, hear, and smell, we have an internal organ that enables us to feel God's presence in all things. God is not in the "God point"; God is everywhere, but this internal organ can sense God's presence and activity in all things and in the whole universe.

The Universe as the Temple of the Spirit

We have now laid out the principal data from which to reflect on the relationship between the Holy Spirit and the universe. First, however, we should emphasize the affinity between our concept of the cosmos as an intricate network of relationships and the Christian understanding of God. Christianity is able, without multiplying the one God, to think of God as a Trinity of divine Persons. These Persons are permanently interrelated, woven together in communion and love, so intimately and completely that they are unified in one God-Trinity.

If God is a relational Reality, it clearly follows that God's creation, the whole universe, also bears the mark of relationality. In the language of quantum physics, "Everything is related to everything, everywhere, at every moment." Everything has been created in the image and likeness of God-Trinity-relationship-communion.

Judaeo-Christian tradition attributes the creation and ordering of the universe to the Father, but more specifically to the Spirit of the Father. The tradition places it at the beginning (Genesis 1:1–2, 2:7) and at the end (Revelation 22:17). In the beautiful words of the Wisdom of Solomon, "The spirit of the Lord has filled the world" (1:7). The Latin word *Spiritus* means breath: "Your immortal Spirit is in all things" (12:1). The Spirit is life and it is *vivicans*, "the giver of life," as we say in the Creed. If that is so, then we can say that the powerful and loving Energy that came before there was a "before," the deep Energy and the Principle that nourishes all things, was always a manifestation of the Holy Spirit.

Indeed the Holy Spirit, because it is God (the Third Person of the Trinity), transcends all representation and existence itself. But its action, which theology calls "the energies of the Spirit," begins in the trinitarian circle and moves outward. Deep Energy is one of its manifestations. The Spirit acted in the "big bang," creating the perfect balance that made possible the emergence of matter, the great red stars, the galaxies and stars of the second and third generation, the planets, the Earth, and the beings that inhabit it, including ourselves.

The Spirit was moving the evolutionary process forward and upward: the process of cosmogenesis, the genesis of the universe that is still becoming and is not yet fully born. It is the Propulsor that pushes everything from behind, and the great Attractor that pulls the universe forward like an arrow, despite the collision of galaxies and massive extinctions of its biotic capital, toward more complex and orderly forms of life.

Since the Spirit is life and the giver of life, it was always present in the life of the bacteria, the plants, the animals, and the human beings in whom God breathed the breath (spirit) of life (Genesis 2:7).

The Spirit was especially present when it "pitched its tent" in Mary, taking up permanent residence in her (Luke 1:35). That is how, by the power of the Holy Spirit (Matthew 1:18, Luke 1:35), the one was born who was later revealed as "the last Adam" (1 Corinthians 15:45), the fulfillment of humanity, Jesus of Nazareth, on whom "the Holy Spirit descended in bodily form like a dove" (Luke 3:22, John 1:32), and who continued to guide and inspire him throughout his life (Luke 4:1, 18). It is the Spirit who raised up Jesus—and thereby made a revolution in evolution, by inaugurating a life without entropy, anticipating the culmination of the cosmogenic process (cf. Romans 1:4; 1 Timothy 3:16). It is the Spirit who initiated the Church at Pentecost, to preserve Jesus' legacy for all peoples (Acts 2:33). It is the Spirit who lives in us as in a temple (1 Corinthians 6:19).

In the words of Jürgen Moltmann, one of the few theologians who has studied the relationship between the Spirit and the cosmos: "God, the Creator of heaven and earth, is present in every creature and in the communion of creation through the cosmic Spirit. God's presence penetrates the whole universe. God is not only the creator of the world, but the Spirit of the universe. By the powers and the possibilities of the Spirit, the Creator dwells in the creatures, giving them life, sustaining their existence, and

leading them toward the future Kingdom. In this sense the history of the universe, of creation, is the history of the effects of
the divine Spirit" (*Doctrina ecológica da criação*, 1993, 33).

"The Spirit Sleeps in the Stone,
Dreams in the Flower . . ."

Christians consider it a sign of faith that the Son of the Father
was incarnate in Jesus of Nazareth, by the power of the Spirit.
We say little or nothing about God dwelling in creation. An old,
anonymous saying expresses it this way: "The Spirit sleeps in the
stone, dreams in the flower, awakens in the animals, and knows it
is awake in human beings." The point is that the Spirit is present
in different ways. It becomes manifest as an explosion of energy,
as matter in movement, as a principle of life, and as an awakener
of consciousness. It inspires great dreams that lead to creativity,
for the Spirit is God's own dream; it builds courage, provokes
holy rage against injustice, inspires a cry for liberation, and acts
as a power of communion and communication.

Being in the universe, the Spirit participates in all the events
in the universe: in the great explosions of supernovas, the collision
of galaxies, the extinction of living species on earth. It rejoices
with creation, suffers with it, cries out with its creatures, sighs
with them for liberation (Romans 8:22–24). The dwelling of God
(*shekinah*) in the temple, representing the presence of the Spirit
among the people, goes into exile with them and returns with
them. The Spirit can even be "quenched" or "grieved" by the
human drama (1 Thessalonians 5:19, Ephesians 4:30).

Remember that one characteristic of the cosmogenic process
is the emergence of complexity, diversity, and the interdependence
of all beings. We have already seen the same characteristics in the
Spirit: the diversity of gifts (1 Corinthians 12:7–11), and at the
same time a relationship of service to all for the common good
(1 Corinthians 12:7). The Spirit moves us toward differentiation
(biodiversity and the diversity of charisms), and at the same time

toward communion and relationship, forming one body, a complex unity (1 Corinthians 12:13).

All these affirmations seem natural in a pneumatological reading of the universe, since everything was created in the Spirit and manifests the presence and action of the Spirit. We are the temple of the Spirit, and the universe—including all its beings, especially human beings—is its field of action.

The Spirit and
the New Heaven and New Earth

The universe is still in a process of genesis, as we are. We are still on a journey through time, moving toward the future, showing what the Spirit has hidden in us, what will gradually be revealed in us through the power of the Spirit. All time is filled with the Spirit: it is in the beginning of creation; it moves upward through all the stages; and it will be there at the end when all beings achieve the fulfillment anticipated in the Mystery. Everything is renewed and revived when the Spirit is poured out on creation, "and the wilderness becomes a fruitful field, and the fruitful field is deemed a forest. Then justice will dwell in the wilderness, and righteousness abide in the fruitful field. The effect of righteousness will be peace, and the result of righteousness, quietness and trust forever" (Isaiah 32:15–17).

That is how the Bible describes the good end of the universe: the moment when the Spirit will prevail over all the divergent and hostile powers of life, and will bring about a new heaven and a new earth (Joel 2:28–32; Revelation 21:1). We will all be drawn together into the dynamic and loving life of the Trinity.

That is the beginning of the true history without entropy, an evolution that penetrates ever more deeply into the ineffable Source of all Being, all Goodness, all Love, that connects and reconnects everything with everything else and with the Source.

In our own time, the interim before the beginning of timelessness, we hear within us the comforting words of Revelation:

"The Spirit and the Bride say, 'Come.' And let everyone who hears [as we do] say, 'Come.' And let everyone who is thirsty [as we are] come. Let anyone who wishes take the water of life as a gift" (Revelation 22:17). *Veni, Creator Spiritus, veni!*

11

The Church,
Sacrament of the Holy Spirit

The second great work of the Holy Spirit was to create the community of the followers of Jesus, the Church. The Church is a complex reality. It is made up of three elements: the historical Jesus, dead and risen; the coming of the Holy Spirit at Pentecost; and its own sociocultural conditioning.

The Death and Resurrection of Jesus:
Preconditions for the Birth of the Church

We cannot imagine the Church without Jesus Christ, but it is not—as we used to say from an ecclesiocentric perspective—the continuation of Christ in history. The Church does in fact continue and deepen the cause of Christ, but it is not Christ; its nature is different from his. Jesus, the man, is God. The Church, being human, possesses elements of divinity but is not God.

There is not a linear connection between Christ and the Church, because the connection between them was broken with Jesus' execution on the cross and with his abandonment by the disciples, except for the women who remained faithful to him.

It was not Jesus' intention to establish the Church, but to proclaim and inaugurate the Reign of God (Mark 1:15, Matthew 4:17). Although Matthew refers three times to the Church (Matthew 16:18, 18:17 and 18), the other gospel writers—Mark, Luke, and John—never use the word "church." Everything is focused on his message of the Reign of God. Jesus "failed" because the people did not accept the good news of the Kingdom, and because Peter betrayed him and the other followers ran away.

In the elegant words of Alfred Loisy (1857–1940, *L'église et l'évangile*, 1902, 111), Jesus preached the Kingdom, but it was the Church that came. Jesus' perspective was apocalyptic and eschatological, assuming the imminent irruption of the Kingdom. "Truly I tell you, there are some standing here who will not taste death until they see that the kingdom of God has come with power" (Mark 9:1). "Truly I tell you, you will not have gone through all the towns of Israel before the Son of Man comes" (Matthew 10:23). "Truly I tell you, this generation will not pass away until all these things have taken place" (Mark 13:30). Jesus also said that only the Father knows the exact time of arrival of the Kingdom (Mark 13:32; Matthew 24:42–44); but he and all the early Christians expected it to come soon, very soon.

Jesus also expressed this expectation with symbolic acts. The gathering of the Twelve symbolized the reconstitution of the twelve tribes of Israel, an eschatological sign well documented by biblical scholars (Ratzinger, *O destino de Jesus e a Iglesia*, 1969, 14). The important thing here is the number twelve, not their identity as Apostles. We see this clearly in Mark's gospel, which speaks only of "the Twelve" (Mark 3:14–16, 4:10, 6:7–35, 9:35, 10:32, 11:11, 14:10–17). Only after the resurrection and Pentecost, with the decision to evangelize the world, are they called the twelve "Apostles," that is, *sent out.*

The Last Supper is another apocalyptic-eschatological sign. Jesus participated in many meals, especially with sinners, as a sign that God's grace and forgiveness are freely offered to everyone. But the Last Supper has a special, eminently eschatological character as a foretaste of the heavenly feast in the Kingdom.

The Church did not yet have an organic connection with the Last Supper, as we know from Luke's narrative. There Jesus says: "'I have eagerly desired to eat this Passover with you before

I suffer; for I tell you, I will not eat it until it is fulfilled in the kingdom of God.' Then he took a cup, and after giving thanks he said, 'Take this and divide it among yourselves; for I tell you that from now on I will not drink of the fruit of the vine until the kingdom of God comes.'" (Luke 22:15–19).

The texts speak for themselves, showing us what Jesus expected to happen. The meal did not become a habitual practice until after the resurrection, Pentecost, and the establishment of ecclesial communities; then it was interpreted and celebrated as the presence of the Risen One, as a reenactment of his sacrificial act and a time of community sharing. That is when it became the Eucharist.

Two things made possible the existence of the Church: the "failure" of Jesus, and his resurrection. He "failed" because he was rejected and executed. If the Kingdom had been accepted there would have been no place for the Church, only for the Kingdom. The Church came later, as a renewal of Jesus' effort to preach the Kingdom and spread his dream to the whole world. But that could happen only because of the resurrection, which showed that he had not really failed. The resurrection was God's answer to Jesus' faithfulness. It was the fulfillment of the dream of the Kingdom in the person of Jesus. He became the complete renewal of the world. The resurrection was like a cameo picture of the good end of God's beloved creation. Thus together, death and resurrection opened the way for the emergence of the Church.

The Historical Birth
of the Church at Pentecost

This vision would remain incomplete, and the Church would not have emerged, if the surprising, mysterious event of Pentecost had not occurred (Acts 2). There the Holy Spirit came down on the frightened community as the Spirit of Christ in the form of tongues of fire, and everyone began to speak in tongues. The Jews and other devout people from different parts of the world heard their strange way of speaking, and came to see what was happening. Parthians, Medes, people from Asia, Egypt, Libya, and other places were amazed to hear people speaking their languages (Acts 2:1–13), and they all understood the same message in their own languages.

Suddenly the confusion of languages, which had begun at Babel when no one could understand anyone else, was overcome. Here there were still many languages, but everyone heard the liberating message Peter was preaching: Jesus was crucified but was now alive, raised up to become the Lord and Christ (Acts 2:36); he had brought reconciliation with God to all who believed in him. Many people were "cut to the heart," converted and were baptized, and they too received the gift of the Holy Spirit (Acts 2:38).

Thus the Church was born through the irruption of the Holy Spirit at Pentecost. For a while the apostolic community remained in Jerusalem, worshiping at the temple. They were surely waiting for the end of time, since an ancient prophecy said that one of the signs of the end would be the outpouring of the Spirit on all flesh; at Pentecost Peter had explicitly cited the prophecy of Joel (Acts 2:16–21; Joel 3:1–5). Pentecost had come upon them as the fulfillment of the old prophecy.

Since they were sure the end was coming soon, it made no sense to have and accumulate worldly goods. They sold their possessions, kept everything in common, and practiced a communal form of consumption (Acts 2:42–45). The author of Acts adds admiringly that there were no poor among them.

Gradually, however, they realized that the end of time was not yet coming. They discovered that time and history still lay ahead of them. It would be the time of the Spirit, time to spread the message of Jesus, the time of the Church. And other things were happening: the difficulty of converting the Jews, the persecution and torture of church members, the martyrdom of James by the sword on Herod's orders (in the year 42, Acts 12:1–6), the arrest of Peter, and especially the surprising conversion of the Gentiles and of a high Roman official, Cornelius (Acts 10). It was time to make a decision: to break away from the small Jewish world and turn to the Gentiles.

But that led to a thorny question: Did they need to retain circumcision (the Jewish equivalent of baptism) as a way of showing the continuity between Judaism and Christianity, or should they set that rite aside and set out on a new, exclusively Christian path? (Acts 15:1–6). The apostles debated the issue at length, in the presence of Paul and Barnabas. At the famous Council of Jerusalem (Acts 15:6–33) they listened to the arguments on each side. Finally they decided "that we should not trouble those Gentiles who are turning to God" (Acts 15:19).

That was when they first spoke the famous words that have echoed through the centuries, whenever the Church is faced with decisions affecting all its members: "For it has seemed good to the Holy Spirit and to us to impose on you no further burden than these essentials" (Acts 15:28). Therefore, the Jewish rite of circumcision would not be imposed on the new Gentile converts; they would become members of the Christian community by conversion and baptism. It was a victory for Christian freedom, the goal advocated by Paul, the prince of the gospel of freedom for the sons and daughters of God.

The Church was becoming increasingly convinced that the Risen Lord is not the one who comes to judge the living and the dead, but the one who went up to heaven, as Luke tells it in the story of Jesus' ascension (Acts 1:6–11). Since the coming of the Kingdom has been delayed, the Church can now look forward and organize itself for mission.

Thus begins a brave process of re-reading the life and work of Jesus. The apostolic community begins to see the Twelve, whose number was important for its symbolism, as the twelve *Apostles* (in Greek, sent out; missionaries). They begin organizing communities and establishing its leadership: "bishops," presbyters, deacons, and other services to the community, many of them charismatic in nature. They bring together the message of Jesus, which was scattered around the different communities (probably in the form of notebooks: a book of Jesus' sayings; a book of miracles; a book of parables; the story of his passion, death, and resurrection; and others). They stitch these materials together, organizing them in themes. Thus we have the four gospels, researched and redacted by people identified as Matthew, Mark, Luke, and John, representing the communities to which they belonged. They begin to celebrate the Eucharist as a way of reenacting the presence of the Risen Lord and his sacrifice of love; they also develop other liturgical celebrations that reflect basic elements of the creed, the identity document of the newly forming community.

Peter and Paul become the leading witnesses to this new reality. Peter, because he was the first to confess faith in Jesus as the Messiah and the Son of God (Matthew 16:16). But let us be clear: the Church was not founded on the person of Peter, whom Jesus once called "Satan" and "a stumbling block" (Matthew 16:23), because of his failure to understand Jesus' destiny as the suffering Servant. Peter's confession of faith had led Jesus to change his name from Simon to Peter; "on this rock I will build my church" (16:18), that is, on this confession of faith. Indeed the best definition of the real, concrete Church is *communitas fidelium*: a community of faith, a community of those who profess the same faith that Peter professed earlier.

Paul was the second great witness. He did not know the historical Jesus (in the flesh), but he had a personal experience of the risen Jesus (in the Spirit), on the Damascus Road where he heard a voice say: "Saul, Saul, why do you persecute me?. . . I am Jesus, whom you are persecuting" (Acts 9:4–5). Without asking anyone else's permission, Paul set out on a great mission, proclaiming especially to the Gentiles that Jesus was the Son of God.

To call Jesus the Son of God, apart from its specific theological content—placing Jesus in the domain of divinity and assuming his direct relationship with the Father, since sonship implies a Father—also carried clear and dangerous political implications, since the emperors claimed to be the sons of "God." To call Jesus the only Son of God meant directly confronting the imperial theology, risking the accusation of the crime of *lèse majesté*. Paul was well aware of this.

After making long journeys around Asia Minor and Greece, Paul went to Jerusalem to meet with Peter and James, the pillars of the early Church. They acknowledged his specific mission. This implied a tacit division of their religious labor: Peter would preach to the Jews, Paul to the Gentiles. But they agreed on one basic doctrine about the meaning of the death and resurrection of Jesus, the Son of God and Savior, and about the action of the Holy Spirit which inspires the communities with its gifts and its enthusiasm.

Luke attributes this bold missionary project to the promise of the Risen Jesus: "You will receive power when the Holy Spirit has come upon you; and you will be my witnesses in Jerusalem, in all Judaea and Samaria, and to the ends of the earth" (Acts 1:8).

In St. Luke's narrative, the centrality of the Spirit gives the Church a universal dimension. It has been sent to people of all languages. This is why in Acts, he lists the twelve different peoples who have heard the message of Christ's salvation in their own tongues. In the oriental worldview, well known to Luke and his audience, every nation is assigned a sign of the zodiac. The people he lists in Acts 2:9–11—Parthians, Medes, Elamites, and so on—correspond exactly, in that order, to the signs of the zodiac. This is Luke's way of expressing the universal dimension of the Church (L. Boff, *Ecclesiogenesis,* 1986).

In fact the Church has the same dimensions as the Risen One and his Spirit, which is always the Spirit of Christ. From this perspective Irenaeus could say: "Where the Church is, there is the Spirit of God; and where the Spirit of God is, there is the Church and all grace" (*Adversus Haereses,* III, 38, 1).

The Church lives by the Spirit; it is the sacrament of the Holy Spirit. Looking closely, as we have done in earlier chapters, the Spirit is at the root of all great works: creation (Genesis 1:1); the formation of the people of Israel, the appearance of political leaders (Judges 13:25; 1 Samuel 11:6); the irruption of fiery prophets (Joel 3); the overshadowing of Mary, the conception of Jesus, his calling at his baptism by John the Baptist, and the sudden outpouring on the community gathered around the Apostles in Jerusalem at Pentecost. It is the Spirit who inspires the decision to go to the Gentiles ("it has seemed good to the Holy Spirit and to us," Acts 15:28), leading to the birth of a universal Church, rather than a "sect of the Nazarenes" (Acts 24:5, 28:22). Later, the Spirit is present in the eucharistic epiclesis, where it is invoked to transform the bread and wine into the body and blood of the Lord.

Charisms:
The Organizing Principle of the Community

In scholastic ecclesiology the physical body of Christ was taken as a metaphor for the Church, the mystical body of Christ. Just as the body has many members with diverse functions, the Church also has many members with specific functions. That was the reasoning of the well-known encyclical *Mystici Corporis Christi* by Pope Pius XII (1943), which compared the visibility, plurality, and unity of the Church with the physical body of Jesus.

This type of ecclesiology does not account for the profound changes undergone by the body of Christ in the resurrection. It was transformed from a physical body into a spiritual body (1 Corinthians 15:44ff.) The spiritual body is the new reality of the risen Jesus, in whom the characteristics of the Spirit are no longer encapsulated in space–time but set free in a cosmic dimension, as Paul says in his letters to the Ephesians and Colossians. Now the cosmic Christ becomes the Spirit (2 Corinthians 3:17), with the characteristics and dimensions of the Spirit which fills the earth and "blows where it chooses" (John 3:8); "and where the Spirit of the Lord is, there is freedom" (2 Corinthians 3:17).

The Church is the body of Christ, risen and spiritualized. If Christ's body is no longer subject to limitations, it follows that the Church as body of Christ cannot be encapsulated in the limited

space of its doctrine, its rites, its liturgy, and its juridical arrange-
ments. It is important to recognize the manifestations of the Spirit
beyond the ecclesial space, in evolution and history—and to grow
with them, daring to become more effective in response to the
inevitable mutations. These manifestations are part of the work
of the Spirit, because the history of salvation is not an alternative
to human history; it takes place within human history.

The Church must learn to see the work of the Spirit in
everyone who lives in truth and love: in social movements, in
the struggle for justice and human rights, in the poor (in the
Pentecost liturgy we call God "the father of the poor"), who
participate in the passion of Christ and yearn to be raised up.
The Spirit is active far beyond the ecclesial space, always ahead of
the missionaries, because it is present wherever people live a life
of love, forgiveness, compassion, solidarity, and care for creation.

If the Church closes itself to the Spirit, it is in danger of hard-
ening, becoming a bastion of conservatism and an instrument of
oppression, and thus denying the vitality of the Spirit.

The Spirit inspires a particular form of ecclesial organization,
different from the classical structure built around the downward
distribution of *sacra potestas* (sacred power) into a few hands, from
the pope to bishops, presbyters, and deacons. That has been the
prevailing pattern, but it has created permanent internal tensions,
because it is based on communal hierarchy rather than communal
equality: "For in the one Spirit we were all baptized into one
body—Jews or Greeks, slaves or free—and we were all made to
drink of one Spirit" (1 Corinthians 12:13). Communal hierarchy
is a contradiction in terms, because communion by definition
rejects hierarchy; it only allows for functional differences that serve
the common good, within the fundamental equality of sons and
daughters of God, brothers and sisters to one another.

For Paul, the Church is a community inhabited by the presence
of the Risen Christ and inspired by the Spirit, a community of
charisms and services. Paul does not think of charism as something extraordinary, but as normal. Charism is simply the role a

person plays in the community for the good of all (1 Corinthians 12:7; Romans 12:4; Ephesians 4:7). There are no uncharismatic members, that is, unemployed, without an assigned role in the community (Romans 12:5–8).

Everyone has equal dignity; there is no room for privileges that would disrupt the community. "The eye cannot say to the hand, 'I have no need of you'" (1 Corinthians 12:21). The golden rule is that "the members may have the same care for one another" (1 Corinthians 12:25).

How different this is from the hierarchical style of organization in which a few people accumulate all the power of voice and decision making, and hand down orders to lay members: "Do what I say, stop asking questions." That would be total control of the head over the feet, the hands over the heart. Unfortunately we forget that the Church is built not only on the Apostles, whose authority came from having lived with Jesus, but also on prophets (Ephesians 2:20) and teachers (Ephesians 4:11; 1 Corinthians 12:28). The hierarchy itself is one kind of charism, for establishing and maintaining unity, but it cannot supplant other charisms, as it often tries to do. That is why we must take Paul's warning seriously: "Do not quench the Spirit" (1 Thessalonians 5:19).

The work of the Spirit in the community is evident in the great "variety of gifts," or charisms (1 Corinthians 12:4–5), expressed in the services listed by the Apostle (1 Corinthians 12:8–10; Romans 12:6–7; Ephesians 4:11–12). Some of these respond to immediate needs, such as the service of compassion (Romans 12:8), exhortation (Romans 12:8), healing and working miracles (1 Corinthians 12:9); others respond to permanent, structural needs that must always be attended to, such as teaching, leadership, and the discernment of spirits (1 Corinthians 12:10; Ephesians 4:11; Romans 12:8). This arrangement gives rise to the Church as a community of brothers and sisters, all seeking the same goals of holiness and witness in a decadent, sometimes hostile world.

This form of organization was not limited to the early Church. We see it today in the Ecclesial Base Communities, where everyone participates and different roles are shared among everyone; also in charismatic groups and the religious life where communion and equality prevail, and differences are seen as riches rather than inequalities.

Unity: One Charism among Others

All kinds of charisms and services exist in the Christian community: "Each has a particular gift from God, one having one kind and another a different kind" (1 Corinthians 7:7), because "to each is given the manifestation of the Spirit for the common good" (1 Corinthians 12:7). All charisms are essential to the Church, but some order is needed among them; otherwise there will be deception, competition, and confusion among them, as Paul warned (1 Corinthians 12:12–31).

Some people speak uncontrollably in tongues, so that no one understands anything. Paul tells them: "In church I would rather speak five words with my mind, in order to instruct others also, than ten thousand words in a tongue" (1 Corinthians 14:19). And they need an interpreter: "If there is no one to interpret, let them be silent in church and speak to themselves and to God" (1 Corinthians 14:28).

To resolve the occasional conflict, Paul offers love as the greatest of all gifts (1 Corinthians 12:31). Those words have become one of the most realistic and profound elegies in all biblical and universal literature: "Love is patient; love is kind; love is not envious or boastful or arrogant or rude. It does not insist on its own way; it is not irritable or resentful; it does not rejoice in wrongdoing, but rejoices in the truth. It bears all things, believes all things, hopes all things, endures all things. Love never ends. . . . The greatest of these is love" (1 Corinthians 13:4–13).

Love is the atmosphere that must infuse all relationships. But love alone is not enough, as Paul makes clear in this text. Without the other virtues, love is reduced to a sentimental feeling instead of a way of life, with openness and acceptance toward everyone.

Every community has to resolve this question: Who can bring cohesion and coordination to the charisms that serve the common good? One charism is needed here, one among others, but different from them: a charism of integration, coordination, and motivation. It is not a charism to be accumulated, subordinating or canceling out other charisms. This charism must be able to synthesize, to bring together, to articulate, to strengthen some people and moderate others who are endangering the flow of community life. This is the function of the charism of directing, presiding, assisting, and governing (1 Corinthians 12:18, 16:16; 1 Thessalonians 5:12; Romans 12:8).

In general we can say that there are no ministries as such in the Second Testament, but only ministers. Thus it sometimes speaks of *episkopoi* (bishops), *presbiteroi* (presbyters), and *diakonoi* (deacons). The bishops, like the presbyters and deacons, are not fundamentally responsible for the sacraments and worship. The role of the bishop, in its original sense, is to observe and arrange the proper functioning of everything in the community. The deacon is an assistant or helper in the leadership of the community. The presbyter is connected to Jewish tradition: a venerable elder, presumably wiser and more prudent, and thus assigned to coordinate the life of the community. The Second Testament uses these worldly terms, signifying mere functions of service, guidance, and leadership—although they seem strange to our ears, which are more accustomed to imperial titles like Monsignor, Reverence, Excellency, or Eminence.

The specific charism of people in positions of leadership, therefore, cannot be to *accumulate*, but to *integrate*. Its purpose is to create the necessary harmony among all the charisms, and thus to generate a rich, complex unity in the ecclesial community.

As we might expect, this essential charism includes others like dialogue, patience, attentive listening, serenity, common sense, and discernment in the face of vanity, self-aggrandizement, or the selfish use of one's gifts. Leaders must be able to admonish, to correct excesses, and to avoid stifling other, simpler and less visible, charisms.

Today this function is practiced in base communities by a coordinator, or even better, by a coordinating team; in the parish by a parish priest; in the diocese by a bishop, and in the universal Church by the pope. Under the charism of unity they are generally the ones to preside at liturgical celebrations, and they are chiefly responsible for the correct transmission of the faith and the coordination of charity. But this function must always be organically related to the community and its charisms, in order not to crystallize, or become autonomous, or degenerate into domination and authoritarianism—the permanent temptation of power.

The Necessary Coexistence of Models of the Church

Unfortunately, this charismatic model of Church did not prevail in history. It remained as a spirit and an atmosphere that understands the Church as a community and communion, reflecting the communion of the Trinity. This spirit remained strong throughout the first millennium of the Church's history, despite its hierarchical structure. Even so, it never became the prevailing model. For reasons we shall not analyze here, the prevailing model conceived of the Church as a perfect society, hierarchical, divided into two bodies: the priesthood and the bishops on one side, and lay members on the other.

They are two strictly different, separated worlds, as affirmed by Pope Gregory XVI (1831–46): "No one can ignore that the Church is an unequal society, in which God assigned some as rulers and others as servants. The latter are the lay people, the former, the clergy." Pius X (1835–1914) raised the wall of separation even higher: "Only the college of pastors has the right and authority to direct and rule; the masses have no right but to be ruled as an obedient flock that follows its shepherd" (L. Boff, *Igreja: Carisma e poder*, 1982, 218). Here the leadership function is confused with division. In a healthy ecclesiology the Church cannot be divided in two; it has two different functions, both of which are expressions of the community and of service to the community.

The Second Vatican Council (1962–65) tried to resolve this problem by thinking first about the Church as People of God (*Lumen Gentium*, chapter II), and only then presenting the hierarchical constitution of the Church (chapter III). But this reversal was canceled out by the curial ecclesiology of the Vatican, supported by Popes John Paul II and Benedict XVI; they gave primacy to the structures of power over those of the communion of all members, thus preventing the eagerly awaited institutional renewal of the Church.

The synod of bishops, episcopal collegiality, and the Pontifical Council for the Laity, all became empty structures with no decision-making authority in the Church. Everything was concentrated in the person of the pope. It was such an enormous, superhuman task that Pope Benedict XVI felt that he lacked the physical, psychic, and spiritual energy to lead the Church. In an act of rare integrity and humility, he resigned from the papacy on February 28, 2013. The election of Pope Francis has brought fresh new air into the Church. Francis sees himself more as the bishop of Rome, presiding with love, than as a pope with monarchical power. He is carrying out a revolution in the papacy, detaching himself from all the symbols of power.

The vision of Popes Gregory XVI and Pius X, mentioned above, is light-years away from that of Jesus, who said very clearly: "But you are not to be called rabbi, for you have one teacher, and you are all [brothers and sisters]" (Matthew 23:8). Or from Paul's liberating words: "As many of you as were baptized into Christ have clothed yourselves with Christ. There is no longer Jew or Greek, there is no longer slave or free, there is no longer male and female [and we might add, clergy and lay people], for all of you are one in Christ Jesus" (Galatians 3:27–28).

The clericalist and exclusivist vision began to penetrate the Church in the year 325, when the Roman emperor Constantine assigned a political role to the clergy, and it was made official in

392 when the Emperor Theodosius († 395) declared Christianity the only official state religion. From then on the category of *sacra potestas* (sacred power) became the structural axis of the whole Church. With the fall of the empire, Leo the Great assumed the title of Pope, which had belonged to the emperors, and gave a strict juridical interpretation to Jesus' words to Peter. This set the future course for the Church as a political power with all its magnificence, royal palaces, and courtly manners. The customary vestments of the emperors—their purple robes, golden staffs, shoulder capes, stoles embroidered with the symbols of power— were now worn by the popes, who against Christ's wishes had become lords of the world.

Now everything would hinge on the sacred power, which would ally itself with other powers in order to strengthen its own. The turning point came in 1075, when Pope Gregory VII († 1085), in his decree *Dictatus Papae* (the dictatorship of the pope), proclaimed himself the bearer of two powers, political and religious. This claim, also made by other popes, such as Eugene III († 1152), was so excessive that St. Bernard († 1153) denounced it, saying that "this Pope is a successor of Constantine rather than Peter."

In effect the popes no longer saw themselves as successors of Peter, the humble fisherman. They became followers of the glorious Christ, completely forgetting the poor Jesus in the manger and the naked Jesus on the cross. Even more, like Innocent IV († 1254), they declared themselves the representatives of God. After that, as if he were God himself, Pope Nicholas V († 1455) in the Treaty of Tordesillas gave Portugal and Spain dominion over the lands and riches of all the world's peoples, known and still to be discovered, with the power to subject and enslave all who refused to accept the Christian faith and acknowledge the sovereignty of their respective kings.

The circle of power was closed when in 1870, under Pius IX, the First Vatican Council declared the pope infallible when he speaks officially on questions of morality and doctrine, with "supreme, ordinary, complete, immediate, and universal power" (canon 331)—in other words, power like God's.

As the hierarchical Church grasped for more and more power, it moved away from the people of God and from the poor. Wherever power prevails, it closes the door to love and mercy. Institutions built on power easily become rigid, inflexible, conservative, and hostile to anything new. All charisms are considered suspect; mystics are closely watched, if not persecuted. Such institutions follow the logic of all power, as Hobbes described it in *Leviathan*: "Power always wants more power, because the only way to protect power is with more and more power."

The tragedy is that this situation has never been challenged, corrected, or placed under the purifying judgment of the Gospel and the practice of the humble, poor Jesus, the persecuted prophet and suffering servant. Thus our hierarchy still upholds and displays royal, courtly manners. It is closer to Herod's palace than to the stable at Bethlehem.

We see that strange, princely splendor in the great celebrations on television, when cardinals and bishops march proudly in their rich and colorful vestments. The scandal is not lost on simple believers, when they compare a sumptuous Christmas Mass in St. Peter's Basilica with the roughness and poverty of the stable at Bethlehem, a refuge for animals, where the Son of God was born.

This contradiction has apparently escaped the notice of the men who consider themselves the successors of the Apostles, no longer humble fishermen, but princes of this world with all the corresponding paraphernalia and palaces. Surely Jesus would never have built his Church on the stone walls of the Vatican, but on the rough bricks of community centers, where the poor come together to hear and meditate on his Gospel.

Today two unequal models of the Church stand face to face: one from high society, pyramidal, hierarchical, centralized, and the other communal, horizontal, decentralized, and egalitarian. The first prays to the glorified Christ, the second to the Spirit, "father of the poor, light of the heart, sweet consolation." The second is closer to the primitive Church, the community of brothers and sisters, followers of the poor and humble Jesus, inspired by the Spirit that is made manifest in the diversity of community services (charisma). This Church is inspired by Jesus' dream, his Kingdom of love, justice, forgiveness, and mercy, fully aware that in his Son Jesus we are all sons and daughters of God.

The other model, the hierarchical pyramid, reflects the historical process through which the hierarchy has passed, always struggling with religious tensions and conflicts (heresies, the confrontation between the Eastern and Western Churches) as well as political ones (imposing and deposing kings and princes, persecuting and being persecuted). This model never experienced the evangelical test of power as service. The outcome of its process was hierarchy (sacred power) rather than the ideal of hieroduly (sacred service) which was upheld by Jesus and the Apostles (Mark 10:42–45; Matthew 23:11), but which was betrayed by the degraded and sometimes corrupt institutional model.

The contradictions have not prevented this model of Church from producing great saints—prophetic men and women, priests, monastics, bishops, cardinals, and even popes with outstanding virtues—who despite the contradictions have lived Jesus' dream of the Kingdom of God and testified to the spirit of the Sermon on the Mount. The gospel and the legacy of Jesus have been preserved, even in fragile and sometimes unclean vessels. We have to claim these flaws as the flaws of our own Church, holy and sinful, because in spite of everything it still shines with the light of Christ and the inspiration of the Spirit.

The model of the Church as communion and web of communities reflects a spirit that always challenges the Church as high society and hierarchy of power, forcing it to measure itself by the practice of Jesus—and despite its limits, to work toward the communion that represents the highest value of faith, the very essence of God the Trinity, the eternal communion of the Father, the Son, and the Holy Spirit. These models coexist, not without tension, but nevertheless without ever undergoing a total, schismatic rupture.

Perhaps in the planetary stage of human history, the future Church will move toward Paul's vision of small communities embedded in different cultures. These communities in turn will acquire their own faces, embrace their differences, and join with other Christian churches and other religions to protect the sacred flame of the Spirit which burns in every human being, in the history of every nation and in all humanity, and—do we dare hope for it?—in the heart of the evolving universe itself. That is the presence of the Kingdom of God in which the Church, in one model or the other, is the sacrament of Christ and of his Spirit, the Church of God.

12

Spirituality

Life according to the Spirit

Christians in the renewed Church, especially in Latin America, have developed their own spirituality for following the life, death, and resurrection of Jesus. To follow Jesus is to enter into his life, take on his Kingdom project, be guided by his practice of unconditional love, especially for the poor, and finally, suffer the same fate that he suffered. This has happened to many people, martyred for their commitment to justice for the poor and to their liberation: lay men and women, religious brothers and sisters, priests, and even bishops.

Now our task is to complete the spirituality of following Jesus with a spirituality inspired by the theology of the Holy Spirit. This is the spirituality that St. Paul called "living by the Spirit" (Galatians 5:16, 25). The Spirit is present and active in everything and everyone, especially where reality is most fragile and life is in danger. Here let us point out some of the ways we see the Spirit acting, beginning with the lessons we learn from the universe.

The Spirit:
The Energy That Infuses and Inspires Everything

As we have seen, many cosmologists—Brian Swimme is an important example—believe that the whole universe and all beings are continually created, infused, and upheld by a mysterious and unnamable Deep Energy. This energy has been described as four great forces: gravitational, electromagnetic, weak nuclear, and strong nuclear. Swimme calls it "the all-nourishing Abyss." It starts before "Planck's wall," the zero point in space and time just before the big bang. We cannot go any further back; we only know what happened after that first, unique beginning. What came "before the before" is what theology calls *Spiritus Creator*, the Creative Spirit.

In spiritual terms this means that whenever we are in contact with any living or inanimate being, we are in communion with the original Energy, without which nothing can exist or survive. But it is not enough to know about this Ultimate Reality; we need to feel it, rejoice in it, revere it, and let it infuse and inspire our bodies and minds. Then we will begin to live a cosmic spirituality, as St. Francis did. He felt that the things around him—the flowers of the field, the birds in the trees and the people he met—were being permanently created and upheld by the Spirit. And he lived this experience in terms of universal brotherhood: Brother Sun, Sister Moon; even wolves and thieves were his brothers and sisters.

With the help of faith and science, we can discern the action of the Spirit in three aspects of the cosmogenic process.

The first is the *complexity* of the single, immense evolutionary process. An infinite number of original energies and particles give rise to an infinite number of beings. The Spirit is poured out in every direction. Reality is not simple but extremely complex, that is, composed of innumerable factors, energies, and elements; being emerges out of the interaction between them. On our blue planet alone, Mother Earth, there are billions and trillions of micro-organisms and living beings: in a word, a wealth of biodiversity.

In terms of spirituality this means that when we open all our senses and let ourselves be touched by this complexity, we are experiencing the diversity of the gifts of the Spirit, the many streams of being and life that flow from this creative wellspring. We are filled with awe and wonder, and sometimes we become ecstatic, speechless, and worshipful.

Interconnectedness is the second aspect of the cosmogenic process that helps us discern the working of the Spirit. All these beings and energies, including the virtual energies traveling through the Higgs field, are not just scattered around space and time. They are all woven together in networks of interdependence, through which they must collaborate in order to coexist and co-evolve.

The elemental particles (hadrons, quarks, protons, neutrons, and others) join together as atoms; atoms become molecules, which become organs, which become organisms, which become bodies and lives; these bodies and lives become kingdoms, species, and so on. Together they form the great cosmic community, dynamic and open to new ways of being.

In spiritual terms: when we contemplate the myriad stars on a dark night; when we are amazed to see different beings harmoniously collaborating, living with others in a mysterious balance; when we observe the multiplicity of cultures, ethnicities, and individuals; then we are overcome by admiration, fascination, and the feelings of joy and awe they produce in us. That is the Spirit, acting in the world and in us.

The third and final characteristic of the universe is *autopoiesis*, that is, its ability to go on expanding, becoming more complex, creating itself as a network of relationships. These relationships were established in the first moment after the big bang, and became more closely woven within the Higgs field, giving shape to complex, increasingly structured orders of being. They reveal a high level of intelligence, and give undeniable evidence of a purpose.

Looking back over 13.7 billion years of energy and matter, we can see the arc of time moving forward and upward. The energy in the universe became matter. Matter became life. Life became individual consciousness. Individual consciousness became collective and planetary consciousness; now planetary consciousness is becoming transcendent and universal. This is why some quantum physicists and other scientists say the universe possesses self-consciousness. There is consciousness in us because it already exists in the universe. In reality we are the part of the Earth that feels, thinks, loves, cares, and worships.

In spiritual terms: whenever we observe complex, organized, meaningful orders of being, whether given by nature or created by human beings to shape their lives and organize their habitat, we are in touch with the Spirit from God that created and ordered the world, as we know from the first lines of the Bible (Genesis 1:1–2). The Spirit opens our heart, stretches our intelligence, and shows us that behind the orders we can see there is an Implicit Order responsible for all the others, as the great physicist and Nobel laureate David Bohm has said. The Holy Spirit is the creator and sustainer of all these orders, explicit and implicit.

The Spirit of Life

"The Spirit is life" (Romans 8:10). The life that comes from the Spirit is most dramatically described by the prophet Ezekiel, when God restores the dry bones to life, saying: "I will cause breath [spirit] to enter you, and you shall live. I will lay sinews on you, and will cause flesh to come upon you, and cover you with skin, and put breath in you, and you shall live" (Ezekiel 37:5–6). Jesus of Nazareth, anointed by the Holy Spirit, went about doing good (Acts 10:38). It was also the Spirit who raised Jesus from among the dead.

To say that "the Spirit is life" means that the Spirit is continually creating and sustaining life, and that the Spirit is constantly beside and within the people whose life is diminished. A large part of humanity, especially in Africa, Asia, and Latin America, live in a world that is alien and hostile to life. For centuries they have been dominated by other nations; they have been robbed of their national resources to support the opulence of the old colonial powers, which in our day have continued as neocolonial powers. There has been a global division of labor: the countries on the periphery, economically poor but ecologically rich, are reduced to exporting "commodities" (raw materials, grains, minerals, water, etc.) without the added value of technological innovation, while they must buy technological products at a high price from the rich countries, which refuse to transfer to them the technology that would give them relative advantage and autonomy. We are talking about a process of neocolonization.

The end result is that those who have been exploited must struggle to survive without the resources for a minimally decent life. They live by struggle with no progress toward liberation.

This poverty does not just happen. It is produced by profoundly unequal social and economic relations which, by increasing the wealth of the rich, generate terrible poverty and injustice for the already impoverished majorities.

In this situation, living by the Spirit means choosing the right to life of the poor. A spirituality that ignores the suffering of the poor is a false spirituality, deaf to the call of the Spirit. However much the faithful pray, sing, dance, and celebrate, unless they are attentive to the Spirit as *Pater pauperum* (Father of the poor), their prayer leads only to self-satisfaction; it does not reach God. The Spirit and its gifts are not in that prayer.

Jorge V. Pixley, a Baptist theologian in Nicaragua, has expressed it well: "Unless the Holy Spirit gives life to those who do not have life, its life-giving power is a lie. In a world that contains a subhuman Third and Fourth World, the spiritual life has more to do with the life of the poor than with the moral athleticism of the believers" (*Vida en el Espíritu*, 1997, 235 and 237).

This is the theological basis of the option for the poor and against their poverty. The Spirit is unfailingly on the side of the poor, quite apart from their moral condition, because they are deprived of life, and the Spirit wants to give them life. But the Spirit has no arms to work with except ours. It is calling us to create the conditions of life for the poor, and for those whose innocent sons and daughters are condemned to die of hunger and the diseases caused by hunger.

Living by the Spirit means struggling for basic human needs, for health, for productive land, for housing, for health care, human security, and basic education. We cannot truly love life and follow the inspiration of the Spirit without defending this cause and suffering for it, in the spirit of the beatitudes. This responsibility cannot be left to the state and its social policies. It is a challenge to all human beings, especially to those who believe in the Spirit of life.

Our commitment to life also gives us thousands of reasons to celebrate life, to sing and rejoice—for instance by ritualizing the struggle in what the Landless Peasants' Movement calls "mystiques," or in community religious celebrations and large public assemblies.

This relates to something we have mentioned before: the dichotomy between spirit and flesh, or between the Spirit and the world. This has to do with both: with life in the Spirit and as a concrete, historically embodied spirituality.

In the biblical perspective "flesh" is not a synonym for the body, because the body is not opposed to the Spirit. Rather the body is the Spirit's place of action, its temple. In biblical terms, "the flesh" is the decadent human situation, the human project hijacked by selfish desires for accumulation and pleasure; it is a lack of solidarity and compassion for those who suffer in this world (compassion is the ability to put ourselves in the place of the other); it is generalized injustice. In short, "the flesh" is human life debased and destroyed by exploitation, humiliation, enslavement (thousands of beautiful women lured into prostitution by promises of employment; children bought, sold, and forced to work; vital organs harvested for sale). "The flesh" produces conflicts, violence, and death. St. Paul says it well: "To set the mind on the flesh is death, but to set the mind on the Spirit is life and peace" (Romans 8:6).

"The flesh" also represents sin. Sin means organizing one's life around the powers of "the flesh," as expressed by wealth, prestige, vanity, an obsession with appearances, superiority through status, beauty, and professional achievement. This self-centeredness is the root of sin, the illusion that one can escape the tribulations of human existence and death. "If you live according to the flesh, you will die; but if by the Spirit you put to death the deeds of the body, you will live" (Romans 8:13).

To live by the Spirit means not falling into the illusions and lies promoted by commercial "marketing"; it means understanding these evils and daring to denounce them, in person and through the groups that defend the rights of the victims. Those who live by the Spirit are no longer slaves to themselves and their individual interests; they open themselves up to others in solidarity, especially toward the people in greatest need. Liberation is not only for me but for everyone, beginning with the most oppressed. This decentering of the self, this turning toward others, is a key feature of the spirituality that is led by the Holy Spirit.

Thus we see the direct opposition between "flesh" and Spirit. They are mutually exclusive projects. The same is true when Holy Scripture speaks of the opposition between the Spirit and "the world." Here, especially in the Gospel of John, "world" does not mean the creation described in Genesis: "God saw everything that he had made, and indeed, it was very good" (Genesis 1:31). On the contrary, "the world" in scripture is a historical and social arrangement not ruled by the logic of the Spirit, but by the dynamic of "the flesh": accumulation through the exploitation of others; devastation of the goods and services that nature provides; the death of biodiversity; social inequality; oppression of the vulnerable by the powerful; ever more lethal weapons and wars, now including drone warfare that not only kills targeted leaders but incinerates hundreds of innocent civilians.

God sent his Son into this "world" to provoke a crisis, according to the Gospel of John, as a way of redeeming it. This world was rescued and renewed by the coming of the Holy Spirit. The world did not accept the Son, but persecuted and killed him. It stifled the Spirit by injustice and by assaults on both human and natural life. We saw Mark's dire warning in chapter 5 of this book: "Whoever blasphemes against the Holy Spirit can never have forgiveness, but is guilty of an eternal sin" (Mark 3:29). It is blasphemy when people recognize the work of the Spirit in

Jesus, but willfully and maliciously ascribe it to Satan. God's forgiveness is always available, but these people are closed to it and
persistently refuse to accept it.

Living by the Spirit means strictly following St. Paul's words:
"I appeal to you therefore, brothers and sisters, by God's
mercy. . . . Do not enter into the schemes of this world, but be
transformed through the renewal of the Spirit" (Romans 12:1–2,
author's translation). A spiritual being seeks transformation, both
personal and structural (*tà skémata* = schemes) by entering into
a different paradigm, living more humanly, respecting the limits
of the planet, producing the bounty that satisfies human needs
but without incurring the devastation of nature.

Such a transformation is not only political. It is an imperative for anyone who wants to live by the Spirit of life. Spiritual
beings are always in conflict with "the schemes of this world,"
that is, with its values, principles, ideals, and purposes; most of
us are oriented to the schemes of "the flesh," which perpetuate
an inhuman status quo, an "evil society" (Paulo Freire) opposed
to life. The epistle attributed to James (who is called "the Lord's
brother" in Galatians 1:19; Mark 6:3 and John 7:3 call him the
Lord's cousin) says wisely: "Do you not know that friendship
with the world is enmity with God? Therefore whoever wishes
to be a friend of the world becomes an enemy of God. Or do
you suppose that it is for nothing that the scripture says, 'God
yearns jealously for the spirit that he has made to dwell in us?'"
(James 4:4–5). It is the power of the Spirit that gives us dreams
and utopias, that inspires us to turn away from "this world" in
order to build another world, both possible and necessary.

The Spirit of Freedom and Liberation

Closely related to the theme of life, which is so easily lost for
the majority of human beings, is the theme of freedom that gives
way to captivity and must be taken back through a process of
liberation. The Second Testament says clearly: "Where the Spirit

of the Lord is, there is freedom" (2 Corinthians 3:17). Much of the life of Jesus, the special bearer of the Spirit, is interwoven with struggle for his people's freedom and liberation.

Jesus freed his people, first, from the image of God as a fierce and unrelenting judge. In its place he proclaimed a kind Father-God, whose principal characteristics are his goodness and mercy even to the ungrateful and the wicked (Luke 6:35).

He also struggled against the prevailing law of his time. The Law was a totalizing presence in the organization of Jewish life, down to the smallest details (Comblin, *O Espírito no mundo*, 62–63). Jesus spoke out vehemently: "For you tithe mint, dill, and cummin, and have neglected the weightier matters of the law: justice and mercy and faith. It is these you ought to have practiced without neglecting the others" (Matthew 23:23).

Living by the Law is opposed to living by the Spirit, for the Law enslaves by "laying heavy burdens on the shoulders of the people" (Matthew 23:4). In its place Jesus offers unconditional love. Everything comes together in freely given love.

Paul understood that lesson and went on: "But now we are discharged from the law [i.e., the system], dead to that which held us captive, so that we are slaves not under the old written code but in the new life of the Spirit" (Romans 7:6). The new Spirit is freedom, because the Spirit is not bound to anything: "It blows where it chooses" (John 3:8). Paul makes a revolutionary claim in his letter to the Galatians, the identity document of Christian freedom: "For freedom Christ has set us free. Stand firm, therefore, and do not submit again to a yoke of slavery" (Galatians 5:1).

Martin Luther took that freedom as the theme of one of the most beautiful texts in Christian theology, *Von der Freiheit eines Christenmenschen* (the freedom of a Christian). Christians are free from everything and everyone, subject to no one, yet out of love they make themselves servants and subjects to everything and everyone. We are free in order to love. Liberation is the act of setting captive freedom free (Comblin, *Vocação para a liberdade*, 1998, all of chapter 9).

The great majorities—people of the African diaspora, oppressed women, indigenous communities, the poor in general—are deprived of the most fundamental freedom: the freedom of survival, food and housing security, safety from environmental disasters. That is what makes their liberation urgent. There is no salvation for the poor in the prevailing system (the law). They are outside, excluded from that law. Then Jesus comes with his manifesto of liberation: "The Spirit of the Lord is upon me, because he has anointed me to bring good news to the poor. He has sent me to proclaim release to the captives . . . to let the oppressed go free" (Luke 4:18). It is by the power of the Spirit that Jesus unleashes this torrent of freedom and liberation.

Living by the Spirit is impossible unless the believer lives in freedom and desires the same for everyone. This freedom, based on the conscientization, organization, and full participation of the oppressed, primarily means taking a stand against the existing system. The system must be overcome within history. But it is also a challenge to churches that have been turned into pharisaic schools of laws and norms that deprive the faithful of their freedom, creativity, and voice. This is a perilous, prophetic struggle because the ecclesiastical authorities, against the movement of the Spirit, have established criteria of exclusivity and punishment that constrain, infantilize, and sometimes excommunicate the faithful.

Living by the Spirit means daring to speak freely and creatively in our celebrations and our initiatives of solidarity and charity. No ecclesiastical credentials are needed, because here, as in the first decisions recounted in the Acts of the Apostles, authority does not come from the apostles (and their successors) but from the Spirit: "For it has seemed good to the Holy Spirit and to us" (Acts 15:28). As Paul told the Galatians, "For freedom Christ has set us free" (Galatians 5:1). Freedom is empty rhetoric unless it is put into practice in our societies, our communities, and our churches.

Christians, especially Catholics, do not know the meaning of freedom in the Church. They listen and obey. Any initiative born of freedom is soon seen as a threat, and placed under vigilance and suspicion. Arbitrarily, for prudential reasons (supposedly so as not to scandalize the faithful), the Christian Base Communities and Bible study groups are suppressed or subjected to limits, norms, and prohibitions that discourage the faithful. Whatever happened to the apostolic principle, "Do not quench the Spirit?"

One moment of great spiritual intensity was the decision by the Latin American Episcopal Conference (CELAM) and the Latin American Confederation of Religious (CLAR), at Medellín in 1969, to make a preferential option for the poor and against their poverty. That option led the bishops to move from the center to the margins, led religious brothers and sisters to insert themselves in the life of the people, and led theologians to take on the cause of liberation for the oppressed. With that act the Church became more spiritual, and thus encouraged Christians to live by the Spirit.

The Spirit of Love

The Spirit is directly connected with the overall process of creation. It is the Energy with which everything began. Love is connected in the same way. After the Spirit comes love, the gift of the Spirit, the cosmic energy that infuses everything, attracts everything, connects and unites everything.

The cosmological and biological basis of love was best explained in the writings of the Chilean biologist Humberto Maturana. He says that love comes into the dynamic of evolution itself from the very beginning. It remains present in every subsequent stage, including the most complex levels of human development. Love gives rise to two kinds of interconnection between individual beings and their environment, one from necessity and the other spontaneous. The first, necessary connections link all beings with each other and with their respective ecosystems, in order to ensure their survival. But there are other, spontaneous connections. The coupling of Higgs bosons, top quarks, and other elementary particles is not necessary for their survival; it occurs out of pure pleasure, in the flow of their life. These are dynamic and reciprocal connections among all beings, animate and inanimate. There is no practical reason for them; they just happen. They represent a unique example of the sheer gratuity of existence. They are like flowers that bloom for the sake of blooming, in the words of the mystic Angelus Silesius.

When such couplings (for example between two protons) create a relational field, love emerges as a cosmic phenomenon. It tends to expand and become increasingly interconnected in living beings, especially in human beings. At our level, unlike that of other beings, it is more than simply spontaneous; it becomes a freely undertaken purpose, which consciously embraces the other and creates love as the supreme value of life.

In this course of events, love emerges as the broader phenomenon of socialization, the love of the many for the many. This is the energy that sustains and gives cohesion to society. Without love, society becomes a forced aggregation, connected by domination and violence, in which everyone is bound to someone else. With the destruction of relatedness and congruence among beings and among human beings, relationships of love and sociability are also destroyed. The love relationship is always an opening to the other, to life together, to communion with others.

The struggle for survival of the strongest does not explain the continuation of life into the present; what sustains life is the love relationship expressed in cooperation and solidarity, beginning with the last and the least. Our hominid ancestors became human by sharing the benefits of their hunting and gathering, and by loving and caring for one another. Language itself, the most distinctive feature of human beings, emerged out of these loving and sharing relationships.

Today as in the past, says Maturana, competitiveness is antisocial; it implies the negation of the other, the refusal to share, the absence of love. The modern, neoliberal, market society is based on competitiveness. As a result it is exclusionary, inhuman, and victimizing. It does not lead to happiness, because it is not governed by relationships of love.

What is different about human love? Maturana replies:"What is specifically human about love is not love as an objective, cosmic and biological phenomenon, but what human beings do with it. Love has to strengthen and deepen our life together, as social beings and beings endowed with language, which reveals our capacity for communication; without love we are not social beings." It is love that makes us human, at both the personal and the social level. Love is the source of fulfillment and happiness. African cultures describe this relationship between the self and the other as *ubuntu*: I can only be myself through other people.

As we have seen, love is a cosmic and biological phenomenon. Among humans it becomes a freely undertaken purpose, a great force of unification, mutual commitment, and companionship. People come together, and through the language of love, they develop feelings of affection and belonging to a shared destiny.

But let us be realistic. Without warm tenderness and without the needed caring, the love relationship is fragile; it does not last, does not grow, and cannot reach out to other beings. Without tenderness and caring, love wastes away. It lacks the necessary environment for the flourishing of what really humanizes: a deep sense of connection to the other, a desire to share, to give and receive love.

This kind of reflection helps us understand the love of God and the Holy Spirit as the unfailing source of love. That is surely the most powerful affirmation in the Second Testament:"God is love" (1 John 4:8, 16). It is profoundly liberating, because it is entirely positive; it does not inspire fear, but rather acceptance and an experience of intimacy with God.

The affirmation comes with important consequences:"Whoever does not love does not know God, for God is love" (1 John 4:8). In other words, without love we seek God in vain. God's name may be always on our lips, and we may proclaim God's existence and providence in beautiful words, but if we do not have love, we are far away from the true God. The God we proclaim is nothing but an idol. This is also the meaning of the Apostle's advice: "Let all that you do be done in love" (1 Corinthians

16:14). To do everything in love means doing it in the context of the Holy Spirit, in the presence of and in communion with the Spirit. To be in the Spirit does not necessarily mean thinking about the Spirit. If we do everything in love, we are objectively in the Spirit. St. John makes that clear: "Those who abide in love abide in God, and God abides in them" (1 John 4:16). Notice that he does not say that those who abide in God abide in love, but the other way around: "Those who abide in love abide in God, and God abides in them." Love is the central criterion, although it may seem redundant to say so, since God is love.

It is the Holy Spirit that leads us to this dimension of love; that is why love comes first on Paul's list of the fruits of the Spirit (Galatians 5:22).

The power of the Holy Spirit is evident in four basic affirmations of the Second Testament: (1) "You shall love your neighbor as yourself" (Mark 12:31); (2) "Love your enemies" (Luke 6:27); (3) "Father, you have loved them even as you have loved me" (John 17:23); and (4) "We are participants of the divine nature" (2 Peter 1:4).

The first affirmation—"Love your neighbor as yourself"—must be understood as an expression of the spirit of Jesus. It's not about loving the person who is physically next to me. Everyone does that; even the wicked love each other. In that sense Jesus was saying nothing new. The newness comes in Jesus' parable of the good Samaritan (Luke 10:30–37): whoever I come near to is a neighbor, regardless of his or her beliefs, ethnicity, and moral condition. It is up to me to make others my neighbors, and to love them as I love myself.

But there is something else new. For Jesus our nearest neighbors, the ones we are called to love, are those whom no one else loves, the strangers, the invisible. The world is full of such people: nameless economic losers who carry no weight in the present system, because they produce very little and consume almost nothing. They are the ones who matter to Jesus. They are the ones we must love as our nearest neighbors, the ones we must love as we love ourselves.

Living in the Spirit means living this universal, borderless love. It means making strangers into neighbors, and neighbors into brothers and sisters—and then truly loving them, from the bottom of our hearts. If Christians showed that kind of love, if they were not so far from Jesus' project of love, there would not be so many invisible, humiliated, and wounded people in our supposedly Christian societies.

Is this the kind of love that our Christian schools and Catholic Pontifical Universities teach their students around the world? They live *etsi Jesus non daretur*, as if Jesus had never lived and taught about love for the most marginalized neighbor. They are leadership factories for our perverse, exclusionary system, the one St. Paul would call the project of "the flesh."

The second affirmation is about love for the enemy. This is a new word from Jesus about love. He is looking for unconditional love, love that transcends all barriers. Indeed there are enemies of life in the world, enemies who do not wish us well, who want to harm us, slander us, and eventually kill us. To include them in our love is the greatest challenge; normally we hate those who hate us, and speak ill of those who speak ill of us. To overcome that instinct, to let ourselves be ruled by the energy of unconditional, universal love that excludes no one, is an act of courage, self-giving, and self-transcendence.

We can never make that leap without the help of the Spirit, who opens our heart to make room for enemies. They are still our enemies, but we do everything we can to avoid harming them or taking revenge. We will not give hatred the last word.

The third affirmation—that Jesus loves his disciples just as the Father loves him—speaks directly of divine love. Out of love for Jesus and the world, the Father sent Jesus to be with us and save us from our material and spiritual misery. He is a source of liberation and uncontainable joy. But this love may also lead us into a "dark night of the spirit." The Father's love led him to deliver his Son to the world (the structures of evil) and leave him on the cross, where he cried out in despair: "My God, my God, why have you forsaken me?" (Mark 15:34). This is the experience of love in the "dark and terrible night" described by the mystics, when they no longer feel God's presence in the midst of an existential inferno.

And yet to love and keep on loving is the supreme expression of gratuitous love. To love for the sake of loving, expecting nothing in return, because love itself is an absolute value. Only the love inspired and sustained by the Spirit is capable of such a spiritual miracle.

This is the logic of living in the Spirit: love is a single movement, from the Father to the Son and to his followers, from the Son to the Father and to his followers. This experience of love inspires feelings of deep gratitude and affection. At the same time it can carry us through an eclipse of God, through the palpable absence of God's love. Yet we must not stop loving, knowing that God goes on loving even out of our sight; knowing that love is stronger than any adversity, for "Love never ends" (1 Corinthians 13:8).

Fourth and finally, life in the Spirit makes possible something ineffable and absolutely mysterious: our participation in the divine nature. This unprecedented affirmation comes in 2 Peter, a letter attributed to the apostle but probably written after his death by one of his disciples, between 70 and 125 CE. The letter says: "His divine power has given us everything needed for life and godliness . . . [so that you] may become participants of the divine nature" (2 Peter 1:3–4). In the Christian understanding, unlike other monotheisms, God's nature is the communion of three Persons and not the separateness of the One. The divine nature is essentially trinitarian. The Father, Son, and Holy Spirit emerge together, none of them prior to the others. They are simultaneous, eternal, and distinct from one another. Their distinctness permits communion and absolute reciprocity among them.

This formulation is different from that of orthodox theology, in which the Father is "the origin and source of all divinity," and transmits it to the Son and the Spirit. We hold that there is no origin and source of divinity, because the Three Divine Persons together are the source and origin; by their nature they emerge as three divine Persons from the beginning and forever.

The trinitarian, relational nature of the divinity is the ultimate basis of love as a cosmic dimension, the cohesive energy behind the creation of diversities and convergences. As beings of love and communion, we are full participants in the trinitarian, communal nature of God. And conversely: because God is trinitarian and relational, all God's creatures reflect this relational, communal nature.

To live by the Spirit means looking at the universe of things, persons, and ourselves from a different perspective. Our very roots are nourished by the nature of God. In some way, we are all made divine. In the words of mystics like St. John of the Cross and Meister Eckhart, "we are God by participation." In this sense, living by the Spirit fills us with dignity and radical respect. When we look at other people and all beings, we see the Triune God emerging within them; we see them as part of the *milieu divin*, the divine environment of which Teilhard de Chardin spoke. In some way we are already in the Kingdom of the Trinity. We cannot yet feel it, but one day this sublime reality will be revealed; then we will fully experience and participate in the triune divinity.

The Gifts and Fruits of the Spirit

The First and Second Testaments use the word "gifts" to describe the presence of the Spirit in the human community and in individuals. These gifts are not something extraordinary but a part of everyday life, when life is lived with justice and with attention to the movement of the Spirit. A gift represents a specific action of the Spirit in the person. The Spirit's self-communication and love surround everyone, but each of us has received some gift, some particular ability or characteristic specifically conferred on us by the Spirit. There are many gifts, but we usually describe them in seven categories. Let us look briefly at each of these.

The gift of wisdom is more than knowledge. Knowledge speaks to our reason. Wisdom speaks to the heart because it engages the senses, sees things from different directions. In the midst of conflicting messages, it helps us recognize which ones make sense; it gives us a sense of measure and balance, which is characteristic of wisdom. People with the gift of wisdom spread serenity, tranquility, and evenhandedness to those around them. A wise person is a good counselor.

The gift of intelligence is the ability to see reality from within, to see its inner meaning. Analytical reason breaks things down into details, atomizes reality; intelligence grasps the whole beyond the parts, and moves from the parts to the whole. Intelligence is reason made perfect, complete, when it is transformed into vision and contemplation. Intelligent people not only know many things, but find surprising connections among them; they are the bearers of *esprit*, that is, they speak a word that enlightens.

The gift of good counsel: Life is complex; sometimes it seems to be made up of opposites. Paths diverge, and sometimes end up in a blind alley or a dense forest. Many people feel confused and abandoned in the midst of conflicting messages, worldviews, and inner feelings. This is the human condition in a world where the Kingdom is always confronted by the anti-Kingdom. The person of good counsel is able to see clearly in a confused situation, to find a way through a complex reality, to discern the right decision and move toward it with assurance. And such a person can share that clear-sightedness with others who come to him or her for help in finding the light. Many people have been rescued from despair and disorientation by a word of good counsel. Few things are more urgently needed in a society that offers so many choices, many of them meaningless and unfulfilling. It is not easy to keep things in proportion and dynamic equilibrium. Too many people fall by the wayside, sad and bitter, lost and alone, without a comforting word from a good counselor.

The gift of courage and strength implies realism in the face of the contradictions, dangers, and threats posed by everyday life. We are often tempted to avoid problems or run away from them in search of false solutions: past experiences that do not fit the present situation, or wishful thinking about the future. We are inundated with self-help programs, pieced together out of psychology, mys-

tical sayings, and everyday common sense. Some are laced with
esoteric advice, horoscopes, and old folktales. In contrast, courage
and strength enable us to confront the obstacles we face without
fear. We sometimes call it resilience: the art of bouncing back,
learning from failure, rising above disappointment. To overcome
discouragement we need "power from on high" (Luke 24:49),
which is how Jesus spoke of the Holy Spirit.

The gift of science: there are many kinds of knowledge. The past
few centuries have been oriented to different fields of science. We
became a knowledge society, which produced many benefits in
everyday life: it has transformed landscapes and improved social
conditions, by improving our health and quality of life. But at the
same time knowledge has been placed at the service of power;
the motto "Knowledge is Power" is inscribed over the doors of
many schools. This power is not used to improve life for everyone, but to accumulate wealth—to torture nature until it hands
over all its secrets, in the words of Francis Bacon, the father of
the scientific method. Tragically it has built a machinery of death
that has devastated nature, waged wars with millions of victims,
and supported the domination of the majority of humanity by
small groups. This kind of science was not consciously designed to
serve life. It chose instead to serve the marketplace, by promoting
the wealth of a few.

But there is another kind of science—a gift of the Spirit—
which uses human reason to understand how nature works, take
what we need from it, and allow it to regenerate. This is science
for the sake of life, for the life of all. Without this science we
would not have begun to understand the complexity of reality,
or to preserve a future of hope for humankind and the Earth.
Science as a gift of the Spirit carries out the messianic mission
of preserving and promoting life.

The gift of piety is very different from what most people think
of as piety: the submissive, obsequious, respectful, prayerful attitude of religious believers. That meaning is also valid, but here
I am referring to a traditional virtue of Roman families, *pietas*.

It is characterized by the love and respect shown by sons and daughters to their parents, especially through prayers and offerings dedicated to the household deities (*penates*). The piety of Roman families helped them avoid quarrels and led to good manners and friendly behavior, especially toward older members and guests of the family. In religious terms, piety expresses a filial relationship of familiarity and intimacy toward God, the Father/Mother who cares lovingly for God's sons and daughters. This piety allays all fears and inspires the trust that we are constantly protected, in the palm of God's hand.

Piety today must also be extended to the Earth and its ecosystems, which are so often impiously exploited. Piety for the Earth, love for it as Mother and Pachamama, sensitivity to the Earth's suffering, would enable it to recover from the wounds we inflict on it. Only if we respect the limits and care for the rhythms of Earth can it go on offering everything we need for life.

The gift of the fear of God: the biblical meaning of fear is similar to what we have just seen of piety. We usually think of fear, even reverent fear, as being afraid. In the biblical understanding, however, fear is synonymous with a reverent, respectful love for God, a loving inclination to submit to God and God's will. We don't play games with God. We don't take God's name in vain, as radio and television personalities do so abusively. We are talking about the Supreme Reality, the reality of love, tenderness, compassion, and mercy. We do not "fear" this God in the same way that we fear the police or a sentence handed down by a strict judge. Rather we respond with reverent, respectful love to God and everything that is God's: the holy Word, the sacraments, religious celebrations, and feast days (Kloppenburg, *Parákletos—O Espírito Santo*, 67–77; Congar, *El Espíritu Santo*, 340–47; Grün, *Confia em tua força*).

Living by the Spirit means internalizing these gifts. They increase the quality of our spiritual lives, because we feel the nearness and the action of the Spirit in the world, in other people, and in ourselves.

In addition to these gifts, we speak of the fruits of the Holy Spirit. They grow out of the vitality and fertility of the Spirit, as fruits grow on the tree. Living in the Spirit transforms a person's life. Such people shine with the virtues that come from immersion in the Spirit, which we also call "the baptism of the Spirit." This baptism does not replace or compete with baptism as a sacrament of Christian initiation. Rather it deepens and radicalizes the presence of the Spirit that was conferred in baptism, as it was when Jesus was baptized by John the Baptist. Then Jesus was filled with the Holy Spirit, and led by the Spirit into the desert to prepare for his mission.

St. Paul lists the fruits of the Spirit in a polemical context, as we have seen, contrasting them with the "works of the flesh" (our deranged lives and uncontrolled passions). He counts fifteen works of the flesh: "fornication, impurity, licentiousness, idolatry, sorcery, enmities, strife, jealousy, anger, quarrels, dissensions, factions, envy, drunkenness, and carousing" (Galatians 5:16–20). Those who live by the flesh "will not inherit the Kingdom of God."

In contrast, he lists nine fruits of the Spirit: "love, joy, peace, patience, kindness, generosity, faithfulness, gentleness, and self-control" (Galatians 5:22–23). These spiritual states are so self-evident that they need no further comment. They are human virtues, which come into action when we live them in full awareness that the Spirit is working in us, guiding our actions.

Wherever the Spirit finds the door open, it comes in and carries out its work of inspiration. Paul concludes: "If we live by the Spirit, let us also be guided by the Spirit" (Galatians 5:25).

The Spirit: Source of Inspiration, Creativity, and Art

So far we have been talking about the Spirit mainly in religious and theological terms. But the Spirit overflows that kind of limits. It is God's own fantasy. It keeps getting ahead of the Church, even ahead of Jesus Christ. It is present wherever people live by love, witness to the truth, act in solidarity, and practice compassion. Wherever such realities are manifest in human beings, anywhere in the world, it is a sign that the Spirit has come upon them and is active within them.

It is by the inspiration of the Spirit that poets and writers redraw life with all its lights and shadows, its dramas and achievements. They are seized by an inner light, and by energies that prompt unexpected connections; they bring something new into the world. Many writers confess, as Nietzsche did, that they feel possessed by an inner energy (a *daimon*, a good spirit) that seizes them and makes them think and write.

By the inspiration of the Spirit, artists and artisans elicit from their material—wood, stone, marble, granite—an image that only they can see in it. The material is spiritualized, and the spirit is materialized. In dance, especially in ballet, bodies are transformed into spirit.

The Spirit is especially intense in music. Sounds are invisible, unconstrained by space and time, just as no one can limit the action of the Spirit. And the melodies they project lift up and penetrate the soul; in them we find comfort, beauty to cry over, soaring joy. The great evangelical theologian Karl Barth used to say that Mozart took his wonderful melodies from heaven and the Breath (the Holy Spirit).

St. Paul talks about the different charismas as human capacities that improve the life of the community, or simply as the in-breaking of the Spirit in the world. He says the Spirit has given to some the gift of words, to others healing, prophecy, the discernment of spirits, knowledge, and wisdom. He concludes: "All these are activated by one and the same Spirit, who allots to each one individually just as the Spirit chooses."

The arts are very much like the Spirit. They are intangible. They are ends in themselves. They have an intrinsic value. They are not a means to other ends, although in their decadent form they may be commercialized and become a source of enrichment. But although they have value, art, music, and poetry in themselves are priceless. They are unique creations, not serial productions. They are like a gift we give to a loved one, valuable for its own sake. Somehow they escape the limits of time and bring us a foretaste of eternity.

Inspiration is in the air and settles on people without regard for their skin color, their social background, or their educational level. How many illiterate artists have emerged in our country, in marginal communities, and were never noticed: poets, artisans, painters, singers, musicians, mystics? Boasting is not the Spirit's way; it is like water that quietly runs along the ground, fills the vessels it is poured into, and always chooses to run downhill.

That is why the Spirit does not have its own figure, as the Father and the Son do. It is portrayed as a dove, but what is important is the radiant light it gives off. It is the Breath (*Spiritus* in Latin) that reveals life, sustains life, and renews life in every way.

The universe and all beings are saturated with Spirit. To recognize its presence in every corner of the cosmos is the work of spirituality, of life in the Spirit.

13

Comments on
Some Hymns to the Holy Spirit

There is a practical purpose behind these theological reflections. The goal is not so much to think about the Holy Spirit,
but to feel the Holy Spirit and to live by the Spirit. The Spirit
by nature is energy, motion, inner movement, enthusiasm, a mysterious power that moves us to act and to resist the demands of
self-importance, pride, and domination by force.

The Spirit works quietly. It shows up in the nooks and crannies of our being. It slowly infiltrates movements of the powerless,
giving them the power of resistance, confrontation, and liberation.
Wherever life is threatened in humanity, in nature, and especially
among the poor, the Spirit intervenes to straighten the bent-over,
lift up the fallen, encourage the hopeless.

This book would not be complete without commenting on some
important hymns from Christian liturgy and popular piety. There
we find the heart of a theology of the Holy Spirit. We don't need
to analyze every verse; Raniero Cantalamessa, the great preacher at
papal retreats, has done that very elegantly with the sequence of the
Pentecostal Mass *Veni, Creator Spiritus* (*O Canto do Espírito*,Vozes, 1998).

The Origin of *Veni, Sancte Spiritus*

This hymn, which is the sequence of the Pentecostal Mass,
is attributed to the Archbishop of Canterbury, Stephen Langton

(† 1228). Langton was born in England, studied in Paris, and became one of the most renowned theologians of his time. He became a close friend of Pope Innocent III (1160–1216), the most powerful pope in the history of the Church. Pope Innocent made him the cardinal archbishop of Canterbury in 1207 while he was still in Paris, but due to opposition from the nobility, he was not able to assume that role until 1213. He is best known for having collaborated in the writing of the Magna Carta, the great monument of political law in England and the world. Also acclaimed for his religious leadership, Langton has been called "perhaps the greatest archbishop in England in the Middle Ages."

This hymn was not originally sung for Pentecost but in the monastic liturgy of the Divine Office (canonical hours), for Terce, or the third hour, which is believed to be when the Holy Spirit descended on the Apostles in the Upper Room (Righetti, *Storia liturgica,* 239). The monks later taught it in churches around the world. It was made a sequence in the Pentecostal Mass by St. Hugh the Great, the abbot of Cluny.

The original Latin text and its translation are as follows:

Veni, Sancte Spiritus,	Come, Holy Spirit,
et emitte caelitus	send forth the heavenly
lucis tuae radium.	radiance of your light.
Veni, pater pauperum,	Come, father of the poor,
veni, dator munerum,	come, giver of gifts,
veni, lumen cordium.	come, light of the heart.
Consolator optime,	Greatest comforter,
dulcis hospes animae,	sweet guest of the soul,
dulce refrigerium.	sweet consolation.
In labore requies,	In labor, rest,
in aestu temperies,	in heat, temperance,
in fletu solatium.	in tears, solace.

O lux beatissima,	O most blessed light,
reple cordis intima	fill the inmost heart
tuorum fidelium.	of your faithful.
Sine tuo numine,	Without your light
nihil est in homine,	there is nothing in the human,
nihil est innoxium.	nothing that is pure.
Lava quod est sordidum,	Cleanse that which is unclean,
riga quod est aridum,	water that which is dry,
sana quod est saucium.	heal that which is wounded.
Flecte quod est rigidum,	Bend that which is inflexible,
fove quod est frigidum,	fire that which is chilled,
rege quod est devium.	correct what goes astray.
Da tuis fidelibus,	Give to your faithful,
in te confidentibus,	those who trust in you,
sacrum septenarium.	the sevenfold gifts.
Da virtutis meritum,	Grant the reward of virtue,
da salutis exitum,	grant the deliverance of salvation,
da perenne gaudium.	grant eternal joy.

Brief Commentary on the Verses

What first catches our attention is the plea, "Come, Holy Spirit." The Spirit always comes; indeed it comes first because it is the Creator Spirit. It was present at the first moment of the creation of the universe, which led to complexity and to life, especially human life; it came to dwell permanently in Mary, formed the holy humanity of Jesus in Mary's womb, and inspired Jesus' whole life and practice. It was also the Spirit that raised Jesus from among the dead.

So why do we pray, "Come, Holy Spirit"? We are asking for the fulfillment of Jesus' promise to the Apostles, to send his Spirit

as a Counselor and Helper (Paraclete, from the Greek *paráklētos*).
Imagine how that first Christian community must have felt: trau-
matized by Jesus' death, unable to understand the resurrection,
subjected to suspicion and persecution by their own Jewish people,
wondering where to turn now.

In this context they recalled Jesus' words: "I will ask the Father,
and he will give you another Advocate (Paraclete), to be with
you forever" (John 14:16). Now they don't need to be afraid: they
have the Holy Spirit to guide and help them with the tasks they
must take up in the wider world.

This could be our prayer today, again and again: "Come, Holy
Spirit." How often we feel we are flying blind, without knowing
where to turn, and yet we have to keep going. How comforting it is
to know that the Spirit will guide us and send us its clarifying light!

Light is the best, most suggestive metaphor for the coming
of the Spirit. It is what we need in our darkest moments; when
we have lost our North Star, the Spirit is a light to show us the
way or at least point in the right direction. If we see even a small,
distant light at such times, we no longer feel so lost: someone
lives there who can take us in.

If we know which way to go, we can find a way there. It may
be stony and full of obstacles, but if we know which way to go,
we can overcome the obstacles with the Helper's power.

It is the poor who feel most lost in this world, without a home
to live in, without knowing where their next meal is coming
from, without a job, without security. Today the poor are a mul-
titude. The poor cry out. And God is the God of their cry, that
is, the one who hears the cry of the oppressed. God sets aside his
transcendence and comes down to hear them and free them, as
he did in Egypt (Exodus 3:7). It is the Spirit who makes us cry
out: *Abba*! Father! (Romans 8:15; Galatians 4:6). That is why we
call the Spirit the father of the poor (*pater pauperum*). He takes
them under his care.

The Spirit doesn't do that in a miraculous sense, but by giving
them courage and resistance, a will to struggle and overcome. It

doesn't let them give up. It has always sent light into the hearts of the poor to help them see viable options, keep struggling, and survive through the ages into our own time. That the native peoples were never completely exterminated, or that the Africans did not perish under the weight of slavery, is because they possessed a power of resistance and liberation. In this hymn that power is called a gift, a light to our hearts, the Holy Spirit.

The Spirit comes in a unique way as a Comforter to the despairing. It doesn't help them from outside. It comes as a guest to live within them, to help and guide them, because that is its mission. In times of great crisis it comes as a bearer of serenity and peace: a sweet consolation.

One important task in this world is to help others and work for their well-being. Work is always demanding and tiresome. The Spirit gives us rest in our labor and shelter from the burning sun. So often the bitterness of life brings us to tears: when we lose a loved one or suffer deep emotional or professional frustration, we seem to fall into an abyss. That is when we cry out: "Spirit, come to console us, dry our tears, comfort our troubled hearts."

At one point the hymn shows something of the nature of the Holy Spirit, by calling it "most blessed light." The word "light" brings us into the dimension of mystery, which neither science nor common sense can explain. We live in the light and under the light, but we never really understand it. Light travels at about 186,000 miles per second, from one end of the universe to the other. Ninety-five percent of everything that exists on earth comes from the light of the sun. It is so mysterious that it can behave simultaneously as a wave and a particle of matter. It can only be fully explained as a mystery. In this it is like the incarnation of the Son of God, the light of the world (John 1:4, 8:12). Just as light is both a wave and a particle, he is both God and man.

We might say that the Spirit is the "most blessed light" that pervades the universe, lifting it up and giving it consistency. This blessed light comes looking for us. It penetrates our hearts with light and warmth, spiritualizes and transfigures us (L. Boff, *Meditacão da luz*). This is its great work: to make us sons and daughters of the light, our lives shining with spirituality.

There is a lot we can do, as intelligent beings and bearers of love and kindness. But we feel vulnerable and broken. There is an unhealed wound in our life. We are like a warped plank that can never be made straight. Why? Perhaps only faith can shed light on that question.

At some point in our life we turned away from the light, from life, and from the call of the Spirit. That rejection became part of our history, and marked us deeply. It did not rob us of the ability to find and love God, but it left us limping, unable to carry out a coherent project of service to others. We stumble, get back on our feet, and fall again. That is the human condition that we all experience in our lives, our philosophies, and our spiritual journeys.

In this sinful condition we need the help of the Spirit, for without it nothing in us is completely pure. We are jointly inhabited by the old Adam and the new Adam. The Spirit strengthens the new Adam in us, so that we can retain a sense of direction for our lives.

The Spirit never stops working. The creation it brings forth is marked by chaos and cosmos, that is, by conflicting dimensions of order and disorder; in human terms, by grace and sin, wisdom and dementia. Some of our behaviors are repugnant, some of our attitudes unfruitful, and on all sides there is sickness of body and spirit. In that context we cry out: "Spirit, come!" Wash away our filth, make us fruitful, cure our sickness.

We still suffer from other weaknesses, and flagrant sins. We are unbending toward others, insensitive to their suffering; we go astray ethically and morally; we lose our inner balance and act hurtfully. Again we seem unable to manage our lives. Then we cry out humbly: "Holy Spirit, come!" Open our hearts to others, help us feel their suffering, make us responsive and caring.

At last we pray for the Spirit to make itself present in its seven gifts, discussed above (wisdom, intelligence, good counsel, courage and strength, science, piety, and the fear of God). These gifts are simply the way the Spirit acts in the different situations of our life.

If we have lived a life of mindful, generous openness to the inspiration of the Spirit, we will have lived a virtuous life. Then we will receive God's recognition (merit), and find the way to salvation (*exitus* = a good outcome, in Latin).

This salvation brings everlasting joy, one of the fruits of the Spirit. But here it means the joy of living without fear, without a loss of energy or vitality. It is the supreme happiness of those who live the life of the Spirit—who share in the Kingdom of the Trinity, Father, Son, and Holy Spirit. As St. Augustine wrote: "It is what the endless end will be, for what other end do we seek but to reach the Kingdom that has no end?" (*City of God*, XXIII). This is the work of the Spirit.

The Origin of *Veni Creator Spiritus*

This is another famous hymn dedicated to the Holy Spirit, sung at Vespers in the Divine Office (canonical hours). It is attributed to Rabanus Maurus (784–856), born in Fulda and appointed archbishop of Mainz. By some unconfirmed sources he was a renowned theologian in the tradition of the Church Fathers (Cantalamessa, 8, 384–87), informally called *praeceptor Germaniae* (teacher of Germany).

Other reliable sources attribute the hymn to an anonymous poet (Righetti, *Storia liturgica*, 3:239). This anonymity appeals to me, because we so often don't know where the Spirit comes from.

These two Pentecostal hymns, the one analyzed above and this *Veni Creator Spiritus*, became the center of a unique popular ceremony in Italy, France, and some other places. Roses, flowers, and confetti were scattered about during the singing. In Rome, Palermo, Siena, and Florence the ritual was practiced even before the feast of Pentecost, on the Sundays after Easter; it was called the Easter of Roses (Righetti, *Storia liturgica*, 2:240).

Doves and other birds symbolic of the Holy Spirit were also released inside the churches. Red ribbons were hung from the cupolas and waved in the breeze for a week. All these rituals emphasized the importance of Pentecost along with Easter and Christmas.

Here is the hymn in Latin, along with a poetic translation from the *Handbook of Christian Feasts and Customs* by Francis X. Weiser, SJ. (1958):

Veni, Creator Spiritus,
mentes tuorum visita,
imple superna gratia
quae tu creasti pectora.

Come, Holy Spirit, Creator blest,
and in our souls take up Thy rest;
come with Thy grace and heavenly aid
to fill the hearts which Thou hast made.

Qui diceris Paraclitus,
altissimi donum Dei,
fons vivus, ignis, caritas,
et spiritalis unctio.

O comforter, to Thee we cry,
O heavenly gift of God Most High,
O fount of life and fire of love,
and sweet anointing from above.

Tu, septiformis munere,
digitus paternae dexterae,
Tu rite promissum Patris,
sermone ditans guttura.

Thou in Thy sevenfold gifts are known;
Thou, finger of God's hand we own;
Thou, promise of the Father, Thou
Who dost the tongue with power imbue.

Accende lumen sensibus:
infunde amorem cordibus:
infirma nostri corporis
virtute firmans perpeti.

Kindle our sense from above,
and make our hearts o'erflow with love;
with patience firm and virtue high
the weakness of our flesh supply.

Hostem repellas longius,
pacemque dones protinus:
ductore sic te praevio
vitemus omne noxium.

Far from us drive the foe we dread,
and grant us Thy peace instead;
so shall we not, with Thee for guide,
turn from the path of life aside.

Per te sciamus da Patrem,
noscamus atque Filium;
Teque utriusque Spiritum
credamus omni tempore.

Oh, may Thy grace on us bestow
the Father and the Son to know;
and Thee, through endless times confessed,
of both the eternal Spirit blest.

Deo Patri sit gloria,
et Filio, qui a mortuis
surrexit, ac Paraclito,
in saeculorum saecula.
Amen.

Now to the Father and the Son,
Who rose from death, be glory given,
with Thou, O Holy Comforter,
henceforth by all in earth and heaven.
Amen.

Brief Commentary on the Verses

"Come, Creator Spirit": This is perhaps the most important prayer that believers can raise to the Holy Spirit. The Spirit is the wind from God that swept over the face of the waters in creation (Genesis 1:1–2), coming and going over the primitive chaos (alternative potentialities), bringing the universe and all beings into existence. In trinitarian terms, the three divine Persons always act together. They all participate in the creative act. But one action is specifically assigned to the Holy Spirit. This suggests, as many cosmologists believe, that the whole universe is the bearer of spirit and consciousness. That makes sense, since the universe emerged from the action of the Spirit, which was present at every stage in the cosmogenic process.

In practical terms, if we consider the creation, the myriad galaxies, stars, and celestial bodies, if we gaze on the immense biodiversity of nature, if we look at human beings in particular, we discover an energy, a movement, and a radiant light that can come only from the Holy Spirit. Our gaze is transfigured. Everything becomes a great sacrament of the Spirit, the holy temple where the Spirit lives and acts.

We invite the Creator Spirit to visit our souls and fill our hearts with its grace. Indeed, the Spirit is the sacred flame burning within us. The prayer awakens our consciousness to this mysterious presence. Once awakened, we can actively celebrate and enjoy its presence. We can affirm a life project always inspired and illumined by the light of the Creator Spirit. We pray that its creative activity will infuse our life projects.

The second verse carries a special theological intensity, seeking in some way to define who the Creator Spirit is for us. It is called the Paraclete, from a Greek word that means Counselor and Helper. It is not just any counselor and helper, but one sent for that purpose by God on High. Its divine character makes it the ultimate counselor, whose counsel and insight are never deceived and cannot deceive us. We can give ourselves trustingly to its guidance. That is why every important gathering of Christians, bishops, cardinals, or papal electors begins with the Gregorian chant of this beautiful hymn, unequaled in its simplicity and harmony.

The Spirit also comes as our Helper. It doesn't do things for us, relieving us of responsibility. Rather, it accompanies us to give us security and courage; it gently infuses our action, improving and completing it. It prevents our practice from becoming corrupted, from straying off the right path.

Who among us feels so omnipotent that we do not need another power, someone to help us, protect us from danger, and save us from failure, when our most cherished projects are going from bad to worse? In these situations we need to trust in the Helping Spirit. That is why the Father and the Son have sent the Spirit to be always with us, beside us, and especially, within us.

The Creator Spirit is a "fount of life." Only dead water comes from a dried-up well. The Spirit is a well of living water. We cannot live without water. Water is holy, part of the essence of life. That is why it can never be a consumer commodity or a source of profit; it is a universal, irreplaceable, essential good, accessible to all living beings, especially human beings.

What a beautiful thing is a backyard well of fresh, living water, flowing day and night! It never runs dry. The Creator Spirit is like that: it always quenches our thirst and assures us of the continuity of life. Water is a symbol of grace, of the living presence of the Creator Spirit.

Fire is as symbolically important as water. It gives light and warmth. It purifies and releases the gold from the dross. Fire gave rise to the universe. The inner temperature of the "big bang" was billions of degrees. All human beings are bearers of a sacred inner flame (the mystic Meister Eckhart called it *Fünklein*), which inspires everything they do and motivates their good works. That is the Spirit in action.

Another name for the Holy Spirit, a sacred name that defines the very nature of the Holy Trinity, is Love. Love is the greatest of all cosmic forces, for it draws everything to it, holds things together, harmonizes, and leads to convergence in the Kingdom of the Trinity. We have said enough about love; no further commentary is needed here. The Holy Spirit as love revitalizes human beings, makes them worthy of being loved, lights up their hearts, and brings them together to help each other, to lighten the burden of existence. When we have love, we have everything.

This verse refers to the spiritual anointing that one receives for a mission. The Spirit is especially present in those who must confront dangers, take on public responsibilities that affect thousands of people, and represent the best of humanity with their charisms and virtues, in order to make God and the message of Jesus credible. Martin Luther King Jr. was anointed by the Holy Spirit to liberate the African Americans who had been denied their civil rights. Gandhi was anointed by the Spirit to liberate India from British colonization. Pope John XXIII was anointed by the Holy Spirit to open the doors and windows of the Church and bring it into the modern world. Dom Helder Câmara was anointed as the great prophet of the poor everywhere in the world. In a deeper sense, everyone is chosen and anointed by the Spirit to live by the Spirit, a life of love, compassion, solidarity, and faithfulness.

The third verse is about the seven gifts we discussed above. We should repeat here that the gifts are the concrete ways the Holy Spirit works in people and in different roles. It is an extension of the powerful, loving hand of the Father.

The fourth verse completes the third. It shows the presence of the Spirit in our minds, awakening us to the mysteries of God. It fills our hearts with love, the greatest of all energies, which moves heaven, the stars, and also our hearts, as Dante said in every canticle of the *Divine Comedy*. How sad, helpless, and absurd life would be if we could not love and be loved! The poet Thiago de Mello said it beautifully: "There is no greater sorrow than that of not being able to give love to the one we love." The Spirit moves people toward each other. All beings are attracted to each other in the gravity of the universe; the same thing is true of human beings.

We are always exposed to illnesses that can weaken or even kill us. In these situations, the Creator Spirit is also revealed as a Helper. We can always call on it and be led by its revitalizing energy.

The human spirit has its own special source of nourishment: the virtues. These are formed by the good habits that we practice and incorporate into our very being, so that they no longer need much effort or even conscious thought; the virtue has been perfected. The Spirit, who is our Comforter and Counselor, is always with us to inspire us in a life of love, patience, peaceful community, solidarity with the last and the least; in short, a virtuous life.

The fifth verse brings us face to face with conflict. In the world there is enmity, injustice, and humiliation. The Kingdom and the Anti-Kingdom are continually confronting one another. We are not facing just any enemy but the archenemy, the great adversary, the bringer of war, the bearer of death: the power of Negativity which is called demonic. The Holy Spirit is stronger than the strong man. It drives far from us everything negative, everything hostile to life.

That is why the Spirit brings the peace we need so much. One of the truest and most objective definitions of peace that I have seen is in the Earth Charter (# 16.4): "Peace is the wholeness created by right relationships with oneself, other persons, other cultures, other life, Earth, and the larger whole of which all are a part." Thus peace is not a specific, self-evident state. It is built through right relationships, which lead to lasting peace. It is not a truce, after which the conflict resumes. Neither is it pacification, the imposition of one side's will over the others. Peace is movement in balance, a web of relationships interwoven to form a world where it is not hard to live as brothers and sisters, where love can flourish and bear fruit. All this is only possible with the help of the universal Helper, the Creator Spirit, the *ductor*, the guide that leads us away from all evil.

The sixth verse is eminently theological. The Holy Spirit helps us know the Son, through whom the Spirit has always worked, and the Spirit and the Son together help us know the Father.

In traditional theology the Spirit proceeds from the Father and the Son; that is, we know it only in its intrinsic relation to the Father and the Son. The divine trinitarian essence and the three divine Persons emerged together from the very beginning, and live together in perpetual communion and mutual self-giving. This is the faith of all Christians and all churches.

The hymn closes with a doxology, a song of praise to the three divine Persons, emphasizing the unique action of the Spirit who raised Jesus and showed him to be the "new Adam," the first fruits of the good end of all creation. Everything ends with an Amen, a total affirmation of everything in the prayer, and the hope that it will endure forever.

This beautiful prayer to the Spirit leaves us filled with peace and serenity, for we know the Spirit has enlightened and inspired everything that we are and everything that we do.

A nós descei, Divina Luz

There is a popular hymn that is often sung in Brazilian churches. It describes the main characteristics of the Holy Spirit and its action in the Church and the world. The text is as follows:

(Refrão): A nós descei, Divina Luz	(Chorus): Come down to us, Divine Light
Em nossas almas ascendei	Set our souls afire
O amor, o amor de Jesus	With love, the love of Jesus
Vós sois a alma da Igreja	You are the soul of the Church
Vós sois a Vida, sois o Amor	You are Life, you are Love
Vós sois a Igreja benfazeja	You are the blessed grace
Que nos irmana no Senhor	That unites us in the Lord
Divino Espírito, descei	Divine Spirit, come down
Os corações vinde inflamar	Come to burn in our hearts
E as nossas almas preparar	Come to prepare our souls
Para o que Deus nos quer falar	For what God wants us to hear

Brief Commentary on the Verses

The Holy Spirit is always associated with light. Light is the most precious, most mysterious reality we know. Only those who have known darkness can appreciate the light. The light from a tiny candle is enough to drive the darkness from a room. That is why we always say the light overcomes the darkness.

Without sunlight, nature loses its energy; human beings grow pale, and we all lose our sense of direction. Almost every religion uses the metaphor of light to express divinity. The scriptures say that God dwells in light inaccessible. Jesus is called the light of the world. The Spirit is the light that transfigures the whole universe.

As the hymn says, the Spirit comes to set our hearts afire with the love of Jesus. Its mission is to extend and complete the work of Jesus. One essential aspect of Jesus' message is unconditional love for friends and enemies, love that knows no boundaries. It is the Spirit that enables us to live that love, so hard to do but so central to Jesus' message.

A church cannot live only by doctrines, moral laws, celebrations, and rules of behavior. More than anything else, a church must be a place to experience the love of our brothers, sisters, and God. It is hard to bear witness to love in a powerful Church, because love disappears when power prevails, even sacred power. Power seldom practices mercy and magnanimity. A community that gives primacy to order and discipline is a community without radiance, without life.

It is love that gives radiance, that attracts and influences people. Unconditional love is irresistible, especially when it takes the form of forgiveness and mercy. Love is the central gift of the Holy Spirit.

Since the Spirit is Love, as the hymn says, it is naturally the soul of the Church. In analytical terms, a Church is the body of the faithful. St. Paul used the metaphor of a body with a diversity of members, each one with a specific function. The body is not a corpse; it has life, it radiates strength, it conveys the joy of existence. The body is animate; that is, it has a soul. The Holy Spirit is its soul.

It is the Holy Spirit that keeps the Church from being just an institution with rules and prohibitions. The community exists with the help of organizational tools. They are not ends in themselves, but means that enable the community to reach people, to fill them with a spirit of devotion, compassion, brotherly love, and constant openness to the Word. When the community bears witness in the world by offering a variety of services, especially to the people in greatest need, if its witness is infused with the love of Jesus and inspired by the Spirit, then it wins everyone's respect and appreciation. The Spirit, which is usually invisible, becomes visible through these actions. The Church becomes a sacrament of the Holy Spirit.

The hymn also says, "You are life." The reality of life is as mysterious as light. We know that life emerged in the cosmogenic process about 3.8 billion years ago. Cosmologists and biologists describe the conditions of that emergence, when universal energy and matter reached a high level of complexity. Life emerged then, as a cosmic imperative. No one really knows what life is. We know that it has interiority, that it lives in constant dialogue with its surroundings, in an exchange of matter and energy that enables life to survive, grow, and reproduce.

Life is so mysterious that all religions have identified God as life and the giver of life. Perhaps life is neither material nor spiritual. It is simply eternal. It comes to us; it gives us life; it brings in death, which allows us to be transfigured and to live in another domain with God, the Fountain of life. It is the work of the Spirit to create, maintain, and transmit life in all its forms (biodiversity)—especially spiritual life, as we have emphasized throughout these reflections.

The hymn also calls the Holy Spirit "blessed grace." Grace and Holy Spirit are synonymous in scripture. Grace is the real, beneficial presence of the Spirit in human beings and in the world (L. Boff, *Liberating Grace*, 1979). Through grace we are made divine in a way; we become "participants of the divine nature," as the Letter of James reminds us.

Theology has always said that there is only an accidental difference between a life of grace on earth and eternal life in glory. They are basically the same. The difference is that here on earth we do not feel grace working in us, except in special situations granted to us by the Spirit; in heaven we are consciously, experientially submerged in grace, that is, in the Kingdom of the Holy Trinity, Father, Son, and Holy Spirit.

The hymn ends by asking the Spirit to keep us always open and alert to "what God wants us to hear." The Spirit does not speak directly into our ears. It awakens us to the signs of the times, the urgent needs of others, the situation of the world, the miserable fate of the poor. God is always sending us messages. The Spirit keeps us alert, because each time it comes is a unique moment. As one of the pre-Socratic philosophers said: "If we don't expect the unexpected, when it happens we will not see it." The Spirit is like that. It is a gentle breeze, not a whirlwind. It is a whisper, not a yell. To hear and understand it we have to be mindful, with open and attentive hearts.

And when the Spirit comes down as Divine Light, it transforms our gaze so that we will recognize its presence in the nooks and crannies of life, bringing us a kind of peace that no medicine can provide. Because the peace that the Spirit gives is the eternal peace of God.

Conclusion

The Spirit Came First, and Keeps on Coming

The Holy Spirit was the first divine Person to come into our history. It came upon Mary of Nazareth; that is, it came to dwell permanently in her (Luke 1:35).

This presence gave rise to the holy humanity of the Son of God. The Word pitched its tent (John 1:14) in the man Jesus, in Mary's womb. At that moment in history, that simple woman of Nazareth became the temple of the living God. Now two divine Persons were living within her: the Spirit, who made her "blessed among women" (Luke 1:42), and the child in her womb, the Son of God.

Later the Spirit came upon Jesus and set him afire for his liberating mission. It came down on the community gathered for the first time in Jerusalem, which became the birth of the Church. It kept coming to other people, whether or not they were baptized Christians, as happened with Cornelius while he was still a pagan (Acts 10:45). Throughout history it was always ahead of the missionaries so that love prevailed, justice was nourished, and compassion lived in the hearts of the people. Once the Spirit had come into history, it never left. It begins with Jesus and moves on from there, but it also declares "the things that are to come" (John 16:13).

Through the Spirit prophets come forward, poets sing, artists create, and people live in goodness and truth. Saints are formed by the Spirit, especially those who give their lives for the life of others.

Also through the Spirit, crumbling institutions are suddenly renewed and begin to serve the communities that need them. The world is pregnant with the Spirit, even though the spirit of wickedness is still working against life and against everything that is holy and divine. The Spirit is invincible.

The Spirit came once, and constantly keeps coming. But in critical times like ours, we need to cry out: "Come, Holy Spirit, and renew the face of the Earth!" Unless the Spirit comes, we will live in the landscape described by the prophet Ezekiel in chapter 37: an Earth covered with corpses and bones. But when the Spirit comes, the corpses are filled with life and the wilderness becomes a garden. The poor are granted justice, the sick are restored to health, and we who are all sinners receive forgiveness and grace.

This is our faith, and more than that, it is our undying hope.

Works Cited

Alday, S. C. *A renovação no Espírito Santo*. Rio de Janeiro: Edições Louva-a-Deus, 1986.

—————. *O Espírito Santo na Igreja dos Atos dos Apóstolos*. São Paulo: Loyola, 1984.

Aranda, A. *Estudios de Pneumatología*. Pamplona: Ediciones Universidad de Pamplona, 1983.

Asciutto, L. "Rapsodia spirituale." In *Nuovo Testamento ci parla dello Spirito*. Brescia: Morcelliana, 1989.

Assmann, H. *A Igreja Eletrônica e seu impacto na América Latina*. Petrópolis: Vozes, 1986.

Balthasar, H. U. "El Desconocido más allá del Verbo." In *Spiritus Creator*. Madrid: Encuentro, 2005.

Barrett, C. K. *El Espíritu Santo en la tradición sinóptica*. Salamanca: Koinonía, 1978. Translated under the title *The Holy Spirit and the Gospel Tradition*. Eugene, OR: Wipf & Stock, 2011.

Basil of Caesarea. *Tratado sobre o Espírito Santo*. São Paulo: Paulus, 1999.

Bergmann, S. *Geist der Natur befreit: Die trinitarische Kosmologie Gregors von Nazianz im Horizont einer ökologischen Theologie der Befreiung*. Mainz: Grünewald, 1995.

Berkhof, H. *Lo Spirito Santo e la Chiesa: La dottrina dello Spirito Santo*. Milan: Jaca Book, 1971.

Boff, L. *Christianity in a Nutshell*. Translated by Phillip Berryman. Maryknoll, NY: Orbis Books, 2013.

—————. *Ecclesiogenesis: The Base Communities Reinvent the Church*. Translated by Robert R. Barr. Maryknoll, NY: Orbis Books, 1986.

—————. "An Ecological View of the Cosmos," in *Cry of the Earth, Cry of the Poor*, 35–62. Maryknoll, NY: Orbis Books, 1997.

—————. *El Ave María: Lo femenino y el Espíritu Santo*. Santander: Sal Terrae, 1984. English translation included in *Praying with Jesus and Mary: Our Father, Hail Mary*. Maryknoll, NY: Orbis Books, 2005.

—————. *El cuidado esencial*, 1999.

——. *El cuidado necesario*, 2012).

——. *El rostro materno de Dios*. Madrid: Paulinas, 1980. Translated under the title *The Maternal Face of God*. San Francisco: HarperCollins, 1987.

——. *Espiritualidad: un camino de transformación*. Santander: Sal Terrae, 2001.

——. *Francis of Rome & Francis of Assisi: A New Springtime for the Church*. Translated by Dinah Livingstone. Maryknoll, NY: Orbis Books, 2014.

——. *Igreja: Carisma e poder*. Petrópolis: Vozes, 1981. Translated under the title *Iglesia: carisma y poder*. Santander: Sal Terrae, 1985, and *Church: Charism and Power*. New York: Crossroad, 1986.

——. *La Trinidad, la sociedad y la liberación*. Madrid: Paulinas, 1987. Translated under the title *Trinity and Society*. Tunbridge Wells, UK: Burns & Oates, and Maryknoll, NY: Orbis Books, 1988.

——. *Liberating Grace*. Translated by John Drury. Maryknoll, NY: Orbis Books, 1979.

——. *Meditacão da luz. O Caminho da Simplicidade*. Petrópolis: Vozes, 2009. Translated under the title *Meditación de la Luz. El camino de la simplicidad*. México: Dabar, 2010.

——. *Saint Joseph*. Translated by Alexandre Guilherme. Eugene, OR: Cascade Books, 2009.

Boff, L., and M. Hathaway. *O Tao da libertação: Explorando a ecologia da transformação*. Petrópolis: Vozes, 2012. In English, *The Tao of Liberation: Exploring the Ecology of Transformation*. Maryknoll, NY: Orbis Books, 2009.

Boff, L., and J. Y. Leloup. *O Espírito na saúde*. Petrópolis: Vozes, 2008.

Boff, L., and R. M. Muraro. *Femenino y masculino: Una nueva conciencia para el encuentro de las diferencias*. Madrid: Trotta, 2002.

Boff, Lina. *Espírito e missão na obra de Lucas e Atos*. São Paulo: Paulinas, 1996.

——. *Espírito e missão na prática pastoral—Acre: 1920–1930*. São Paulo: Paulus, 1997.

——. *Espírito e missão na teología—Um enfoque histórico-teológico 1850–1930*. São Paulo: Paulus, 1998.

Bourassa, F. "Dans la communion de l'Esprit Saint." *Science et Esprit* 34, no. 1 (1938): 31–56.

Bouyer, L. *Le Consolateur et vie de grâce*. Paris: Du Cerf, 1980.

Brandt, H. *O risco do Espírito. Um estudo pneumatológico*. São Leopoldo: Sinodal, 1977.

Bulgakov, S. *Il Paráclito*. Bologna: Dehoniana, 1971.

Cacciatore, O. G. *Dicionário de cultos afro-brasileiros*. Río de Janeiro, 1977.

Cantalamessa, Raniero. *O Canto do Espírito*. Petrópolis: Vozes, 1998. Translated under the title *El Canto del Espíritu*. PPC, 1999.

Casaldáliga, P., and J. M. Vigil. *Espiritualidad de la liberación*. San Salvador: UCA, 1993. Translated under the title *Political Holiness*. Tunbridge Wells, UK: Burns & Oates, and Maryknoll, NY: Orbis Books, 1994.

Caselles, H. "Saint Esprit. Ancient Testament et Judaisme." In *Supplément au Dictionnaire de la Bible, IX*. París, 1991.

Comblin, J. *A força da Palavra*. Petrópolis: Vozes, 1986.

———. *O Espírito Santo e a libertação*. Petrópolis: Vozes, 1987. Translated under the titles *El Espíritu Santo y la liberación*. Madrid: Paulinas, 1987, and *The Holy Spirit and Liberation*. Tunbridge Wells: Burns & Oates, and Maryknoll, NY: Orbis Books, 1989.

———. *O Espírito no mundo*. Petrópolis: Vozes, 1978.

———. *O Espírito Santo e a tradição de Jesus* (posthumous publication). São Bernardo do Campo: Nhanduti, 2012.

———. *O povo de Deu*. Paulus, 2002.

———. *O Tempo da Ação. Ensaio sobre o Espírito e a história*. Petrópolis: Vozes, 1982.

———. *Vocaçao para a liberdade*. Paulus, 1998.

Congar, Y. M. J. "Blasphemy Against the Holy Spirit." *Concilium 99: Experience of the Spirit* (1974), 138–51.

———. *El Espíritu Santo*. Barcelona: Herder, 1991. Translated under the title *I Believe in the Holy Spirit*. New York: Crossroad, 1997.

Corten, A. *Le pentecôstisme au Brésil. Émotion du pauvre et romantisme théologique*. Paris: Karathala, 1995.

Cox, H. *Fire from Heaven: The Rise of Pentecostal Spirituality and the Reshaping of Religion in the Twenty-First Century*. New York: Addison-Wesley, 1995.

Dalbessio, A. *Lo Espirito Santo—Nel Nuovo Testamento, nella Chiesa e nella vita del cristiano*. Milan: Ed. San Paolo, 1994.

Dalmais, J. H. "L'Esprit de vérité et de vie: Pneumatologie grecque et latine: Opposition ou complémentarité." *Lumen Vitae* (1972): 572–85.

Diaz, J. "Espírito Santo." *EB* 6 (1971): 622–29.

Drouot, Patrick. *O físico, o xamã e o místico* (2001) 60–73.

Duhm, H. *Die bösen Geister im Alten Testament*. Tübingen: Mohr, 1904.

Dunn, J. D. C. *Baptism in the Holy Spirit: A Re-examination of the New Testament Teaching on the Gift of the Spirit in Relation to Pentecostalism Today*. London: SCM Press, 1970.

204   *Works Cited*

————. *Jesus and the Spirit: A Study of the Religious and Charismatic Experience of Jesus and the First Christians as Reflected in the New Testament.* London: SCM Press, 1976.

Elbein, J. "A percepção ideológica dos fenômenos religiosos: sistema nagô no Brasil, negritude versus sincretismo." *Revista Vozes* 71 (1977): 543–54.

————. *Os nagô e a morte.* Petrópolis: Vozes, 1976.

Evdokimov, P. *L'Esprit Saint dans la tradition orthodoxe.* Paris: Du Cerf, 1969.

Fabri dos Anjos, M. *Sob o fogo do Espírito.* São Paulo: Soter/Paulinas, 1998.

Fierro, N. *Hildegard of Bingen and Her Vision of the Feminine.* Lanham, MD: Rowman & Littlefield, 1994.

Flanagan, S. *Hildegard of Bingen 1098–1179: A Visionary Life.* London: Routledge, 1998.

Freyer, T. *Pneumatologie als Strukturprinzip der Dogmatik: Überlegungen im Anschluss an die Lehre von der "Geisttaufe" bei Karl Barth.* Paderborn: Schöningh, 1982.

Galindo, F. *El fenómeno de las sectas fundamentalistas: La conquista evangélica de América Latina.* Estella: Verbo Divino, 1994.

Galot, Jean. *L'Esprit Saint, personne de communion.* Parole Et Silence, 1997.

Giesriegl, R. *Die Sprengkraft des Geistes: Charismen und apostolischer Dienst des Paulus im 1. Korintherbrief.* Thaur/Tirol: Wort und Welt Verlag, 1989.

Grün, A. *Confia em tua força—os sete dons do Espírito Santo.* Petrópolis: Vozes, 2011.

Hasenhütl, G. *Charisma, Ordnungsprinzip der Kirche.* Freiburg: Herder, 1969.

Hawking, Stephen. *A Brief History of Time.* New York: Bantam Books, 1988.

Julian of Norwich. *Revelations of Divine Love.* London, 1952.

Kloppenburg, B. *Parákletos—O Espírito Santo.* Petrópolis: Vozes, 1997.

Koven, J. *History and Spirit: An Inquiry into the Philosophy of Liberation.* Boston: Beacon Press, 1991.

Ladaria, L. F. *El Espíritu en Clemente Alejandrino.* Madrid: UPVM, 1980.

Lyonnet, S. "Le récit de l'Annonciation et la maternité divine de la Sainte Vierge." *L'ami du clergé* 66 (1956): 33–46.

Mambrino, J. "Les deux mains du Père dans l'oeuvre de S. Irenée." *Nouvelle Revue Théologique* 79 (1957): 355–70.

Maturana, Humberto. *El árbol del conocimiento.* 1995.

Moltmann, J. *Doctrina ecológica de la creación—Dios en la creación.* Salamanca: Sígueme, 1987. Translated under the title *God in Creation.* Minneapolis: Fortress Press, 1993.

————. *El Espíritu de vida.* Salamanca: Sígueme, 1998. Translated under the title *The Spirit of Life.* Minneapolis: Fortress Press, 1992.

Monod, Jacques. *Chance and Necessity.* Translated by Austryn Wainhouse. New York: Knopf, 1971.

Montague, G. T. *The Holy Spirit: The Growth of Biblical Tradition.* New York: Paulist Press, 1976.

Mühlen, H. *Einübung in die christliche Grundrfahrung,* vol. 1: *Lehre und Zuspruch;* vol. 2: *Gebet und Erwartung.* Mainz: Grünewald, 1976.

————. *El Espíritu Santo en la Iglesia.* Salamanca: Secretariado Trinitario, 1974.

————. *Erfahrung und Theologie des Heiligen Geistes.* Munich: Kösel, 1974.

————. *Iniciación a la experiencia cristiana fundamental,* 1976.

————. *Renovación de la fe Cristiana: Charisma, espíritu, liberación,* 1974.

Novaes, R. R. *Os escolhidos de Deus: Pentecostais, trabalhadores & cidadania.* São Paulo: Ed. Marco Zero, 1985.

Nouwen, H. *Formación Espiritual: Siguiendo los impulsos del Espíritu.* Santander: Sal Terrae, 2011. In English *Spiritual Formation: Following the Movements of the Spirit.* San Francisco: HarperCollins, 2010.

Oro, A. P. *Avanço pentecostal e reação católica.* Petrópolis: Vozes, 1996.

Piaget, Jean. *The Child's Conception of the World.* Translated by Joan Tomlinson and Andrew Tomlinson. New York: Harcourt, Brace, 1929.

Pikaza, X. *El Espíritu Santo y Jesús.* Salamanca: Secretariado Trinitario, 1982.

Pixley, J. V. *Vida en el Espíritu: El proyecto mesiánico de Jesús después de la resurrección.* Managua: CIEETS, 1993.

Prigogene, Ilya, and Isabelle Stengers. *Order Out of Chaos.* New York: Bantam Books, 1984.

Richard, J. "Conçu du Saint Esprit, né de la Vierge Marie." *Église et Théologie* 10 (1979): 291–323.

Righetti, M. *Storia liturgica.* 3 vols. Rome: Ancora, 1956.

Robinson, H. W. *The Christian Experience of the Holy Spirit.* London: William Collins, 1962.

Rolim, F. C. *Anjos, demônios e espíritos.* Petrópolis: Vozes, 1998.

————. *O que é pentecostalismo.* São Paulo: Brasiliense, 1997.

————. *Pentecostalismo: Brasil e América Latina.* Petrópolis: Vozes, 1995.

Rossato, P. *The Spirit as Lord.* Edinburgh: T & T Clark, 1981.

Salado Martinez, Domingo. *La religiosidad magica: Estudio critico-fenomenologico sobre la interferencia magia-religion.* Edit. San Esteban, 1980.

Sanchis, P., et al. *Nem anjos nem demonios.* Petrópolis: Vozes, 1994.

Santa Ana, J. *Die politische Ökonomie des Heiligen Geistes: Zeitschrift europäischer Christen.* Bremen, 1990.

Schiwy, G. *Der Geist des neuen Zeitalters: New Spirituality und Christentum.* Munich: Kösel, 1987.

Schnackenburg, Rudolf. *Cristologia do Novo Testamento.*

Schütz, C. *Introducción a la pneumatología.* Salamanca: Koinonía, 1991.

Schweizer, E. *El Espíritu Santo.* Salamanca: Sígueme, 1984.

Secondin, B. *Nuovi cammini dello Spirito.* Roma: Ed. Paoline, 1990.

Silva, Andréia Cristina. *Hildegarda de Bingen e as sutilezas da natureza de diversas criaturas.* Rio de Janeiro: Instituto de Filosofia e Ciências Sociais: UFRJ, 2002.

Sobrino, J. "El Espíritu, memoria e imaginación de Jesús en el mundo." *Sal Terrae 966* (1994): 181–96.

Sofiati, F. M. *Religião e Juventude.* Aparecida: Idéias & Letras, 2011.

Swimme, B., and T. Berry. *The Universe Story.* San Francisco: Harper San Francisco, 1992.

Termolen, R. *Hildegard von Bingen Biographie.* Augsburg: Patloch Verlag, 1990.

Tillich, Paul. *Systematic Theology.* 1951–63. Chicago: University of Chicago Press, 1967.

Tylor, E. B. *Primitive Culture.* New York: Henry Holt, 1877.

Van der Leeuw, J. J. *El fuego creador.* Barcelona: 1928.

———. *Phänomenologie der Religion.* Tübingen: Mohr, 1956.

Various authors. *Vem Espírito Santo e renova a face da Terra. Seis estudos bíblicos.* São Paulo: CEDI/CMI, 1990.

———. *Renovação Carismática Católica: uma análise sociológica e interpretações teológicas.* Petrópolis Vozes/INP/CERIS, 1978.

———. "Holy Spirit: Mystery and History." *Concilium* no.148 (1979).

———. "The Experience of the Spirit." *Concilium* no. 99 (1974).

———. *O Espírito Santo: pessoa, presença, atuação.* Petrópolis: Vozes, 1973.

Verges, S. *Imagen del Espíritu de Jesús.* Salamanca: Secretariado Trinitario, 1997.

Volz, P. *Das Dämonische in Jahwe.* Tübingen: Mohr, 1924.

Weil, P. *A consciência cósmica.* Petrópolis: Vozes, 1999.

Weisser, Francis X., SJ. *Handbook of Christian Feasts and Customs.* New York: Harcourt, Brace, 1958.

Welker, M. *O Espírito de Deus: Teologia do Espírito Santo.* São Leopoldo: Sinodal & EST, 2010.

Westermann, C. "Geist im Alten Testament." *Evangelische Theologie* 41 (1981): 223ff.

Zohar, D. *La inteligencia espiritual.* Barcelona: Plaza & Janes, 2001.

Index